Acknowled

Grateful acknowledgement is made for re_
book: in Chapter 1 a table from 'Defining Bullying For A Seconuary schoo.
by C.M.J. Arora and D.A. Thompson, in *Education and Child Psychology,* 4,
3, 1987, two tables in Chapter 2 from Olweus, D. (1988), 'Bully/Victim problems
among schoolchildren', in J.P. Myklebust and R. Ommundsen, (eds.),
Psykologprofesjonen mot ar 2000: Arbeidsliv, internasjonalisering og utdannelse.
Also for the reproduction of the poem 'Back In The Playground Blues' in Chapter
10 from Rosen, M. (1985) *Kingfisher Book of Children's Poetry,* publisher
Kingfisher Books.

Cover designed by:
Anne Marie Forster

The address of Professional Development Foundation is
21, Limehouse Cut, Morris Road, London E14 6NT.

The Professional Development Foundation

The Professional Development Foundation is a non-profit research trust limited by guarantee and registered in England. (No. 2172915)

It specialises in the promotion of practitioner generated research. Through a network of advisors in higher education and other professionals it provides consultancy, research support and professional development programmes. Both independent projects and cooperative schemes with other professional and academic institutions are undertaken. It assists with the publication of work relevant to the promotion of professional development.

21 Limehouse Cut
Morris Road
London E14 6NT

Contents

List of Contributors

Sue Askew   Part-time Lecturer, Institute of Education, University of London
Part-time Teacher, Hackney Downs Boys' School, ILEA

Maurice Chazan   Emeritus Professor of Education, University College of Swansea

James O. Hammond   General Secretary, National Confederation of Parent-Teacher Associations

Graham Herbert   Head of Year, Saladine Nook High School, Huddersfield

David A. Lane   Director, Professional Development Foundation, London
Formerly Director, Islington Education Guidance Centre, London

Ken Reid   Reader in Education, West Glamorgan Institute of Higher Education, Swansea

Erling Roland   Principal Lecturer, Stavanger College of Education, Norway
Research Director of follow-up study: Norwegian Campaign Against Bullying

Dave Smith   Senior Educational Psychologist, Durham

Pete Stephenson   Specialist Educational Psychologist (Children in Care), County of Cleveland

Delwyn P. Tattum   Reader in Education, South Glamorgan Institute of Higher Education, Cardiff

Wendy Titman   Freelance Consultant and Trainer in Childhood Issues

Geoffrey Walford   Lecturer, Strategic Management and Policy Studies Division, Aston University, Birmingham

Foreword

It is with some trepidation that I set out to introduce a very important book because bullying in schools is something of which I am fortunate enough to have no experience since neither of my children was subjected to it — as far as I know, and that is an important caveat.

No parents can ever be totally confident that their children will escape bullying. Nor can they place hand on heart and say they have never worried about the possibility. Most parents have enough confidence in the school to think that any problem of this kind will immediately be communicated to them by caring teachers. But will it?

The fact is that most bullying in schools goes undetected for the very good reason that the victims are too terrified to report their suffering for fear of reprisals which can often be brutal. The characteristics which typify a child who is being regularly bullied are known to us all. There will be a marked lack of enthusiasm to go to school; younger children will display extreme reluctance to leave their parents at the school gate; homework may be left undone because this gains attention from the teacher; on questioning, the child becomes evasive and shifty; sleeplessness is often a giveaway. All these can be manifestations of the acute anxiety resulting from persistent bullying. Once a child has fallen foul of the menace, and demonstrated that he will not 'split', the bullying becomes more intense and the ensuing terror increases.

Undoubtedly, the parent feels compassion for the victims and wants only to protect loved ones from further suffering. But it is also legitimate to ask questions about the bullies who inflict that suffering. What is it that drives them to the point where they clearly derive some perverse pleasure from watching their victims squirm? Is there some deep-seated psychological problem which needs exposing and treating?

I think there most certainly is. The role of the educational psychologist should be paramount in helping children who bully others. These children unquestionably fall into the category of those who have special needs and it is a tribute to the authors of this book that they both recognise this and provide an in-depth analysis which shows parents a way forward which could help them to face the future with a greater degree of optimism than they might have been able to muster hitherto. Of course it is possible to move forward only when the bullying tendency has been discovered. Treatment can only be commenced after detection. This means that methods must be devised which lead to early discovery. Accepting that the victim will generally be an unwilling communicator, it is necessary for skilled observation to be available as soon as teachers suspect bullying. This assumes that training courses will include elements which will allow teachers both to detect early signs of bullying and to communicate their concerns to parents and psychologists in a non-threatening way which will allow them to work together in the interests of both victim and persecutor. It may well be that in some extreme cases, other more severe action such as suspension, is appropriate and this should be implemented without hesitation when no other course of action has produced beneficial results.

I have also found it instructive to read in this book of the way bullying can be dealt with through the curriculum. Parents will be fascinated by this account and will perhaps be forgiven for displaying a degree of scepticism about its efficacy. This illustrates very well the basic difficulty we all have in understanding what it is that drives the bully on, and how much more difficult it is to rely on the school's natural learning processes to eradicate these unfortunate tendencies. On the other hand, many parents will have sympathy with a commonsense approach which suggests that some bullying at least must have its origins in disaffection. If schools fail to provide a curriculum relevant to the needs of the particular youngster, then it is not too difficult to make some connection between Boredom and Bullying, the latter being an outlet for frustration stemming from irritation with all that the whole pointless school scene represents. This is perhaps what has led to the success of initiatives like the Technical and Vocational Education Initiative (TVEI). It has captured the interest of a whole range of students who might otherwise have found their attention wandering and has resulted in both pupils and parents being immensely impressed with the way in which skills on working together and solving problems have been developed. It is profoundly to be hoped that the proposed National Curriculum will not be so narrow that it will disaffect many young people in both primary and secondary stages.

So little do we understand of what makes the bully tick that it would be right to encourage research into the causes. If it has been found useful in Scandinavia to proceed in this way, there must be lessons we can learn, and it is perhaps not too much to expect those who control these matters to provide a degree of funding to increase our understanding of the problem and thus to move towards eradicating it.

I have no hesitation in recommending this book. It is an important contribution to the debate about bullying in schools and provides much to interest all those who are in a position to increase the early detection and sympathetic caring of both bully and victim. This will need a concerted effort from teachers, educational psychologists, parents and, perhaps most of all, from other children, who are the first to observe what is happening.

James O. Hammond

Chapter 1
Violence and Aggression in Schools
Delwyn Tattum

Introduction

Bullying is the most malicious and malevolent form of deviant behaviour widely practiced in our schools and yet it has received only scant attention from national and local authorities. It has failed to claim the attention of teachers' unions; our schools have given it low priority compared with disruptive behaviour and truancy; and finally, it has been ignored by the educational research community. Yet, all who work in education will agree that it is widespread and persistent. The following chapters show that the perpetrators are to be found in nursery classes, infant, junior and secondary schools, and their conduct includes name-calling and teasing; jostling and punching; intimidation and extortion; and even assault, maiming and murder. The victims for their part suffer the physical and psychological abuse of their persons, isolation and loneliness, insecurity and anxiety arising from the threatening atmosphere which surrounds them. At its most insidious it focuses on vulnerable children who are regarded as being different because of their ethnic origins, homosexual inclinations, or, physical or mental disabilities. It is difficult to understand why bullying has not been taken seriously. Schools are civilized, caring places where anti-social behaviour is condemned and dealt with by teachers. Can it be that it is seen to be an inevitable part of school life, or that it is a necessary part of growing up, or that it is so secretive that it defies the vigilance of teachers?

But bullying affects those other children who may witness the violence and aggression and the consequent distress of the victim. It may adversely affect the atmosphere of a class and even the climate of a school — consider the instance at Burnage High School where a 13 year old boy was stabbed to death when he went to the assistance of others who were being bullied. What is more, less aggressive pupils can be drawn into the taunting and tormenting of victims by group pressure and other social psychological factors. They too know how quickly the direction of the attack can change, for you cannot intimidate and oppress one person without making all others afraid. Children have a basic right to freedom from pain, humiliation and fear, whether caused by adults or other children. Schools have a responsibility to create a secure and safe environment for children who are in their care so that parents may hand their children over in the confident knowledge that they will be protected from the bullies.

Although teachers are acquainted with the problem, there is a need to heighten professional awareness and this the book aims to do. It also aims to answer a number of questions. How extensive is the problem? What are the characteristics of the pupils involved? What factors contribute to bullying in schools? How can we minimize the problem? These and other issues are addressed, and one theme is that schools *can* reduce the problem behaviour once staff acknowledge that it is a problem. There are schools with good and bad records in tackling bullying (Stephenson and Smith, Ch. 4) and other contributors describe a range of strategies which they have successfully used in schools and on in-service courses.

The incidence of bullying

As already indicated, research into bullying has been a neglected area in the United Kingdom. In fact, most of the early research was indirect and incidental. For example, Lowenstein (1975) in his study of violent and disruptive behaviour, links bullying with 'malicious destruction of property, and attacks by pupils or parents on members of the school staff'. Other reports on indiscipline similarly fail to isolate bullying from other forms of disruptive behaviour, for example, HMI (1978) associate it with fighting, assault, loud and aggressive behaviour. In an attempt to categorize different forms of indiscipline, the Pack Report (1977) defined pupil-pupil aggression as 'bullying, intimidation, violence, assault, extortion, theft'; they then proceed largely to ignore bullying, devoting just a paragraph (2.53) to it in their chapter on truancy. More recently, the Northern Ireland report on Discipline in Schools (1987) follows the Scottish formula and provides a list of 7 categories of disruptive behaviour, one of which is 'bullying, intimidation, extortion and theft'. What is disturbing from this report is that bullying was the offence for which corporal punishment was most frequently applied. Primary school returns identified it in 16 per cent of cases and in secondary schools the figure was 20 per cent. These figures are supported by STOPP's data for the UK in general. These data raise two points: that schools are able to identify bullying from other forms of pupil behaviour and that the response to violence was further *legitimate* violence in many cases. Considering the latter point one might ask whether institutionalized violence actually helps individuals to condone their own violent conduct? Also, do teachers as 'bullies' present models which support pupils as bullies? Askew (Ch. 5) considers this possibility with particular reference to the aggressive male ethos prevalent in boys' schools.

One of the difficulties associated with gathering accurate data on the incidence of bullying is that it is a secret activity, therefore, researchers have relied on self-reports and accounts from other pupils, teachers and parents. From their longitudinal study of child-rearing, Newson and Newson (1984) reported that out of a sample of 700 eleven year olds, the mothers of 26 per cent were aware that their children were being bullied at school, 4 per cent seriously, and another 22 per cent were being bullied in the street. Stephenson and Smith (Ch. 4) also present high regional figures using self-report and teacher ratings. They found a high measure of agreement between the two groups and a figure of 23 per cent of their 1,078 sample of final year primary school pupils were identified as being involved as either victims or bullies.

In a study of a small comprehensive school, in which the staff did not believe that bullying was a major problem, Arora and Thompson (1987) drew upon pupils in the first three years (12-14 year olds) to indicate the frequency of occurrence and to provide a working definition of bullying. Their summary findings are reproduced in Table 1 which indicates a relatively high incidence of some items.

We note that 50 per cent of 14 year olds reported that someone had tried to kick them at least once during the previous week and 36 per cent of the same group indicated that someone had tried to break something that belonged to them. Most disturbing, all groups reported extortion — 19 per cent of 12 year old boys presenting the highest figure.

Table 1: Percentages of boys and girls reporting incidents defined as 'bullying' to have happened *once or more than once* during the previous week. (Arora and Thompson, 1987)

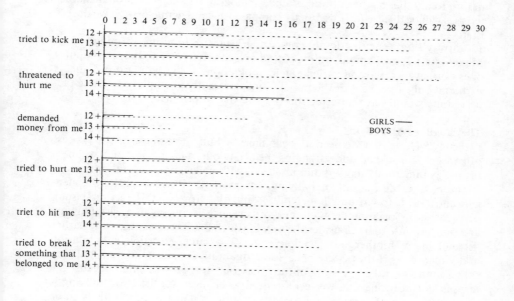

It is important that we note the lower incidence of bullying among the 13 year olds. Arora and Thompson speculate about possible explanations and suggest that one reason may be 'the effects of a good pastoral care system in that particular year, which happened to have a year tutor who was particularly concerned to establish harmonious relationships between the children'.

As the UK data on how much bullying there is in our schools is so limited, it is not possible to generalize with confidence. Therefore we must turn to researchers in the Scandinavian countries who have conducted a number of national surveys over the last decade or so. A summary of their work is given by Roland (Ch. 2) and he writes that *at least* 5 per cent of children are victims and a similar number do the bullying. Most readers would probably regard countries such as Denmark, Finland, Norway and Sweden as civilized, law-abiding communities, and therefore would accept the application of these figures to the United Kingdom. The latest school population figures for maintained primary and secondary schools in England, Scotland and Wales in 1985-86 give a total of 8,378,000 pupils. A five per cent calculation would present 436,900 pupils involved in bullying and a similar figure suffering as victims. Some Scandinavian research would place the percentage of victims at 10% which would represent about 870,000 unhappy, anxious and fearful children. If we accept these figures, then these children constitute the largest group of children with special needs in the country.

There is certainly a need for research on a national scale to ascertain the extent of the problem because it is never satisfactory to transpose data from one nation to another as the cultural, social, demographic and educational characteristics will be different. If we briefly compare England with Norway, we oberve that:
1. Norway's largest cities do not compare in size with London, Birmingham or Manchester; 2. a 600 pupil limit is placed on schools in Norway; 3. the country does not have a large and varied ethnic population; 4. the standard of living is high and only 4 per cent of the population is presently unemployed. These factors alone would have an effect on the size of the problem.

The language of bullying

It may well be that we need a vocabulary of bullying as part of the process of conceptualising and understanding the behaviour; a language which will help people as they think about it and discuss it with colleagues. Several other contributors offer definitions of bullying, for example, Roland (p.21), Stephenson and Smith (p.45) and Lane (p.95), and therefore in this section I shall consider the association between the words we use in conjunction with bullying and our response to it. Consider the way in which the Reports referred to earlier list bullying with other anti-social acts such as assault, extortion, intimidation and violence, as if these were behaviours qualitatively different from bullying rather than integral expressions of the behaviour. It is probable that because the term is so embracing that we feel the need to be more specific; for bullying is on a continuum of severity and so our response to name-calling is likely to be different from hearing about extortion. But the point that we need to appreciate in each instance is that bullying is a wilful, conscious desire to hurt another person.

In August 1987 I was invited to give a talk on a Council of Europe course on bullying in Norway. One point of interest to emerge from the gathering of representatives from fifteen European countries was that the Scandinavians were the only nations to have seriously tackled the problem, although all accepted that it happened in their schools too. The Spanish and Portuguese teachers explained that whilst they understood the behaviour and had observed it, they did not have a specific word to name it. In Scandinavia it is called 'mobbing' (Roland Ch. 2 explains the origin of the word) which in English carries a group or gang connotation. In America it is called 'victimization' which, interestingly, changes the focus of attention away from the bully to the victim. And whilst they use victimization to include attacks on teachers and property, it is a most valuable reversal of attention because it could bring about a more sympathetic response from adults who may dismiss bullying with asides like — 'Boys will be boys'. 'It goes on everywhere'. 'It's part of growing up'.

Bullying is a complex problem and it may be that one of the reasons why we have not given it greater attention is that we hold too simplistic a view. Some of the elements which need to be included in a deeper appreciation of the behaviour are:—

1. Nature — it can be physical and/or psychological.

2. Intensity — ranging from horseplay to vicious assault.

3. Duration — the bullying can be occasional and shortlived or it can be regular and longstanding. Children have been systematically bullied for several years.

4. Intentionality — bullying is premeditated and calculated rather than thoughtless or accidental.

5. Numbers — it may be carried out by one child or by a gang.

6. Motivation — Roland (Ch. 2) maintains that with boys the motive is mainly personalized power but with girls it has more to do with affiliation, as the victim is excluded, scapegoated, as part of preserving group solidarity.

In addition to the complexity involved in understanding the behaviour itself there are what Olweus (1984) calls a 'theory sketch of factors of potential significance for whipping boys (victims) and/or bully problems'. These factors are divided into 4 sectors and are aimed at obtaining a preliminary overview of the complex of problems and at making sure that essential aspects are not neglected in empirical investigations. An appraisal of the relative importance of these sectors is presented in subsequent chapters.

A. School setting — size of school and class, teachers, group climate.

B. External characteristics of potential victims and bullies — physical handicaps, obesity, language problems, physical strength and weakness.

C. Psychological/behaviour characteristics of victims and bullies — attitude to violence, aggression, degree of anxiety, self-esteem etc.

D. Socio-economic
   background —   home conditions, child-rearing.

Finally, there is need to distinguish between violent behaviour *against* another and aggressive behaviour *between* children. Teachers can differentiate between bullying and fighting. Dierenfield (1982), in his survey of 465 teachers working in comprehensive schools, found that 37 per cent regarded 'physical violence to other pupils' to be a serious or moderate problem, and 45 per cent thought 'aggressive behaviour among pupils' to be a seriour or moderate problem. Similarly, evidence would indicate that teachers and peers are able to identify, with a high degree of agreement, which children are bullies and which are victims (Stephenson and Smith, Ch. 4; Olweus, 1984). In his study of delinquency, West (1973) also reported high correlations between teachers' and peer ratings of aggressive behaviour, and that the best predictor of delinquency was their combined ratings of troublesomeness or persistent misconduct. From previously unpublished data from David Lane, disruptive behaviour linked with bullying may well be an even more accurate predictor of violent behaviour in adolescence and adulthood. From a 5 year study of a sample of 200 pupils from various secondary schools, 50 were randomly sampled who were disruptive but *not* bullies and 50 who were *both* disruptive and bullies. In the first group, 17 (4 girls, 13 boys) received convictions totalling 33 offences of which 4 involved violence towards other persons, but in the second group 31 (5 girls, 26 boys) received a total of 162 convictions of which 22 per cent (36) involved violence.

The subject of the violent personal histories of bullies is dealt with in greater detail by Lane (Ch. 9), but the link between child aggressive behaviour and adult violence is another important reason why we should take the problem of bullying much more seriously.

The second part of this chapter will be devoted to considering two aspects of bullying not discussed elsewhere in the book: anxieties about transfer from primary to secondary school and racial harassment. Finally, some recommendations will be given to help parents, teachers and schools in general tackle and reduce the incidence of victimization.

Transfer from primary to secondary school

The subject of institutionalized bullying as in prefectorial and fagging systems is dealt with by Walford (Ch. 7) in his consideration of the public school tradition, as is the matter of initiation rites of passage which induct new members. But before dealing with the anxieties of 11 year olds it is appropriate that institutionalized violence in the military be briefly considered because it involves both initiation and racial bullying. Army bullying became a public issue in 1987 because of the revelations of cruel and degrading conduct against young recruits, which were proved at courts-martial. The humiliating ordeals suffered by some soldiers shocked the public and posed serious questions for the Ministry of Defence.

12

Accusations of ill-treatment were rife following the suicide in January, 1987, of Jeffrey Singh, a junior soldier in the Infantry Battalion at Shorncliffe, Kent. A reporter in the *Guardian* (24 January, 1988) wrote, 'A coroner's court heard that Singh had been subjected to an amount of racial abuse but no bullying'. This statement indicates a total lack of understanding of what bullying entails. Other incidents involved violent initiation ceremonies of new recruits by soliders in the 1st Battalion, The King's Own Scottish Borderers, and also the extreme measure of the commanding officer of the 2nd Battalion, the Coldstream Guards, placing his 550 men under something approaching house arrest until one of them revealed who was responsible for a second attack on a 21 year old recruit.

The army projects a tough, macho image which is seen as part and parcel of the military philosophy of turning youngsters into men, but it is an approach which can be misused by bullying men. Jack Ashley, MP, in a House of Commons debate, developed this point as he warned of the dangers inherent in putting such a philosophy into practice.

We all want and need tough, well-trained, disciplined soldiers. We are proud of the Army, but we have to recognise that the power structure of the forces and the type of training required to produce tough soldiers create fertile soil for bullying. Officers, commissioned and non-commissioned, rightly demand an automatic response to authority. The close community life within units creates an admirable *esprit de corps,* but at the same time it readily breeds intolerance of individualistic behaviour or of someone who is felt to have let the side down. These are vital factors in army life, but they are reasons for vigilance against bullying, not for acceptance of it.

(*Hansard*, 26 January, 1988)

Schools are not closed, military establishments but they are authoritarian, and boys' schools in particular do create an aggressive atmosphere which may be seen to condone pupil-pupil aggression — see Askew (Ch. 5) for a fuller treatment of this theme. Elsewhere (Tattum, 1982) I have presented an analysis of the nature of an aggressive school ethos within the dimensions of legitimate and illegitimate violence; direct and indirect violence; public and private violence.

Research evidence demonstrates that pupils about to transfer from primary to secondary school face the prospect with mixed feelings of excitement and apprehension. They face the challenge of their new school with a feeling of anticipation and in most cases they settle down quickly and without too much fuss — but that does not mean that they do not have worries and fears. Davies (1986) compiled the anticipations of 155 pupils in their last 2 weeks of primary school and found that when they wrote about their worries the most commonly mentioned was the fear of being bullied (58.1%), followed by concern about specific subjects (36.8%). The prominence given to bullying is confirmed by Galton and Wilcocks (1983), who found that, together with separation from friends, it was the major concern. In two samples, one rural and one urban, Youngman and Lunzer (1977) studied 1,500 children in transition and found that most anxiety revolved around having things stolen, losing items, school work and examinations, and bullying. Measor and Woods (1984) also name 5 major anxieties — the size and more complex organisation of the new school, new forms of discipline and authority, new work demands, the possibility of losing one's friends, and the prospect of being bullied.

Most commentators express the view that the majority of pupils quickly adjust, with a gradual decline in their anxieties and fears, but Brown and Armstrong (1982) maintain that it is more a matter of changes in the nature of their worries as they settle into the school's routine. A sample of 173 pupils in a girls' secondary school were asked to write an essay about their feelings on coming to their new school. Using content analysis, 22 worries were itemized and these were given in the form of a questionnaire to the same girls during the latter part of their second term. Not surprisingly, worries about school routines and feeling lost declined markedly, but worries about tests increased from 2 per cent to 81 per cent of the sample. Fear of being bullied also increased in term two from 5 per cent to 30 per cent.

As bullying figures so prominently in the worries of new pupils it is obvious that a single session on the subject in a tutorial period is inadequate. Tutors should return to the topic discretely on a regular basis; tutor groups should be encouraged to talk amongst themselves about the transfer and their gradual adjustment; and tutors need to create a talking-listening relationship to encourage pupils to approach them with their worries. Feeder schools may well supply the names of potentially vulnerable individuals with some history of being bullied so that tutors may be watchful for signs of distress, absenteeism or deterioration in school work. Management can also devise schemes whereby older pupils are made responsible for the well-being of the new intake.

Racism and bullying

The Army is not the only institution in which racial bullying occurs and, because of an increasing number of disturbing reports from schools and colleges throughout the country, the Commission for Racial Equality conducted a survey in 1985 to assess the incidence of racial abuse and violence. Their report, *Learning in Terror* (1988), contains the following extract in the Foreword:

> Racial harassment is widespread and persistent — and in most areas very little is done about it. Young people in schools and colleges suffer no less than men and women on the streets and in their own homes on housing estates. As in the wider environment, their walls may be daubed with the same threatening symbols of hatred and oppression. Acts of aggression and outbreaks of violence are not uncommon.
>
> The perpetrators span the age range from infant to adult, and they include pupils, students, teachers, lecturers and parents, all of whom may be described as ordinary, everyday members of the learning community. We need to disabuse our minds of the idea that racial harassment is solely or even mainly the work of the lunatic fringe or outside extremist.
>
> (Aaron Hayes, CRE Chief Executive)

Although the Report places racial harassment in the wider context of racial discrimination, it is concerned about the insecurity and anxiety suffered by the victims and gives a number of graphic, illustrative cases of hurtful and vicious things said and done by teachers as well as pupils — below are 3 selected examples:—

> The decision was taken to leave the district by a couple in a small country town in the Home Counties. The mother is German and the father Cypriot. Their 13 year old daughter was subjected to a strange combination of epithets: 'Nazi' in relation to her mother and 'Wog' and 'Paki' in relation to her father. The child and her mother had also been attacked in their home by stone-throwing youngsters from the school. The school response was poor, and the police advised the family to move away.
>
> (Case B)
>
> At a primary school in the North-West a black child was forced by the teacher to stand up and spell out the word 'golliwog' when the child refused to read it out in class because he found it offensive.
>
> (Case D)
>
> A young Sikh published his own account of the regular verbal and physical harassment that he had experienced in the seven years he had spent at schools in the South. Much of that harassment was directed at his hair and turban, both regarded as sacred symbols. Sometimes teachers would join in or even initiate the jokes. The main effect, he said, was to erode his self-confidence and capacity to concentrate on learning.
>
> (Case J)

In 1984 the DES published *Race Relations in Schools* in which it commented on the widespread nature of racial harassment and the need for whole-school policies supported by local and central government, in order to improve the skills of teachers in dealing with incidents and in promoting genuine equality of opportunity in school. At the same time the message was reinforced by the Secretary of State for Education, Sir Keith Joseph, in a speech on 'Racial Bullying in Schools', in which he said that effective learning could take place only when pupils had a feeling of self-confidence, well-being and security flourishing in conditions conducive to equality of opportunity, mutual respect and cooperation.

The wider implications of racial abuse are eloquently made in the Swann Report: *Education for All* (1985):

> We believe the essential difference between racist name-calling and other forms of name-calling is that whereas the latter may be related only to the individual characteristics of a child, the former is a reference not only to the child but also by extension to their family and indeed more broadly their ethnic community as a whole.

The problems faced by ethnic minorities in schools has also been well documented by Eggleston et al. (1986).

As is the case with bullying in general, very little research has been carried out in this area of racial bullying in schools but the advice of Government Departments is that LEA's issue guidelines to schools on the identification of incidents and procedures to deal with them, and schools themselves must monitor incidents and devise a policy for all staff and pupils. The tragic events at Manchester's Burnage High School in 1986 sharpens the urgency with which schools and colleges must address these matters. Amhed Ullah, a 13 year old Asian boy, was murdered in the playground of Burnage school by a white teenager, Darren Coulburn, who had a history of disruption and bullying. Manchester City Council commissioned an inquiry but at the time of writing only 11 of its 33 chapters have been released because the Council claims it could be sued for defamation by persons named. The inquiry panel of four has much to say which goes beyond racial harassment to encompass all forms of discrimination and bullying. The team found that Burnage's governors and senior management were wholeheartedly committed to anti-racist policies; yet the school had been the scene of great racial conflict and polarization of its students. The found the theoretical model applied by the head had placed racism in 'some kind of moral vacuum totally divorced from the more complex reality of human relations' in class, school or community. It was a model which ignored the existence of other forms of discrimination, harassment and abuse, such as by social class, sex, age or disability. In essence the school's policy was too narrowly conceived, with the result that it failed to create a genuinely caring and supportive ethos which sought out injustices however they manifested themselves. The panel concluded that anti-racist policies can work if the entire school and community are involved in drawing them up and in implementing them — this is equally true of anti-bullying policies. Parents, pupils and staff need to share in the responsibility for the well-being of the school and its members.

In a report commissioned by the MacDonald inquiry into the Burnage murder, Elinor Kelly (Kelly & Cohn, 1988) reports on her survey into pupil perceptions of racial violence in three Manchester secondary schools. In her study she examined two aspects of bullying — name-calling and fighting, and reports a disturbing gap between pupil complaints and teacher response, which suggests that communication between pupils and teachers is not good when it comes to this form of behaviour. Expressions of discontent came from children of Celtic and European origin as well as black/asian pupils; and they were not commenting on individual and inter-personal behaviour in isolation but, more seriously, about racial victimisation which has 'the potential or actuality of group formation which could flare into inter-racial conflicts'.

In Kelly & Cohn (1988) the subject of name-calling and teasing is reported on by Cohn in a study of six schools (3 primary, 3 secondary) in an outer London Borough. Her findings demonstrate that:

(1) Of all names cited, the 'racist' names were the most prevalent and the most varied.
(2) The amount and variety of 'racist' name-calling increased with age.

(3) The amount of 'racist' names from boys of all ages was greater than from girls of similar age.

(4) The attitudes towards name-calling differed according to both age and gender.

Cohn describes the ethos of one school, where home and school work together to counter the adverse effects of racial harassment. She maintains that teachers have to choose between being silent and acquiescent and speaking out. Ethnic origin is a convenient way of categorising, evaluating and reacting to one another, and children will treat others with respect or as inferior as they hear them described in complimentary or uncomplimentary terms in society in general and school in particular.

Comments and guidelines

The following guidelines attempt to draw together the main conclusions and recommendations of the other contrbitors to this book. They are not presented as a rigid, stepwise programme but as a sequencing of actions which may be seen to be appropriate by schools.

It is the case that most bullying takes place where teachers cannot directly intervene. Therefore we need strategies which approach the problem by an alternative route, the aim of which is to change attitudes towards bullying and at the same time create a school ethos that will not tolerate the oppression of one member by another. The aim must be for a whole-school policy which is consistent with the daily experiences of teachers, pupils and parents. Where bullying is reported by pupils or parents, it must be taken seriously and acted upon in a way which discourages the bully without humiliating the victim. Both parties in their interactional roles need help and the school should devise a whole-curriculum and extra-curricular programme to change attitudes and behaviour.

This is not a total plan to reduce bullying, because its nature is complex and our understanding of the problem is partial. Before we can effectively begin to cope, we need to acknowledge the prevalence of bullying and understand more fully its origins and nature. This is the first book in the United Kingdom devoted entirely to bullying and it is hoped that it will stimulate discussion and inquiry in a neglected area of schooling.

1. A school may need to heighten the awareness of its teaching and non-teaching staff so that they are more alert to and sensitive about bullying. The short-term and long-term implications are too serious for staff to adopt a 'head in the sand' attitude. A survey may be necessary to convince some teachers about its prevalence and frequency of occurrence.

2. Parents should be invited to a school and/or a class meeting — in primary schools a class meeting could be more effective as it is most closely associated with parental concerns. This meeting should precede any policy statement as parents should be involved in its development.

3. Senior management and governors should devise a whole-school policy aimed at consciously creating a caring, concerned, sympathetic ethos in which all members are respected. Do the principles of justice and fairness operate through the school? What emphasis is placed on rewards compared with sanctions? Is the school characterized by a highly competitive ethos?

4. The policy should involve parents and the wider community as bullying takes place also en route to and from school.

5. The subject of bullying can be tackled through both the pastoral and academic curriculum. There is extensive resource material available to supplement existing pastoral programmes and most departments should be able to introduce suitable material into their syllabuses for different age groups.

6. Opportunities need to be made for groups to discuss bullying and role-playing situations devised so that pupils learn to cope better with bullies. Similarly, bullies need to be placed in situations which require them to see things from the victim's position.

7. Research confirms that teachers and peers are able to identify victims and bullies accurately. This information should be gathered so that staff may act early to prevent bullying histories from developing.

8. The school's physical environment and general organisation should be examined and likely bullying places supervised more closely.

9. Victims need their self-esteem raised through social skills classes; they also need support from teachers and parents to counter their feelings of inferiority and even guilt. Parents may need to be advised on how they may help their child.

10. Bullies too need help to show them that they can satisfy their needs through working with others rather than in conflictual and competitive ways.

11. Other agencies should be involved at each stage and especially in the work with individual pupils and their families.

Acknowledgement
I wish to thank David Lane for kindly supplying me with unpublished data from the Professional Development Foundation data base.

References
Arora, C.M.J., and Thompson, D.A. (1987). Defining Bullying for a Secondary School. *Education and Child Psychology*, 4, 4, 110-20.

Brown, J.M., and Armstrong, R. (1982). The Structure of Pupils' Worries During Transition from Junior to Secondary School. *British Educational Journal*, 8, 2, 123-31.

Commission for Racial Equality. (1988). *Learning in Terror! A survey of racial harassment in schools and colleges*. CRE, London.

Davies, G.T. (1986). *A First Year Tutorial Handbook*. Blackwell.

Department of Education for Northern Ireland. (1987). *Report of the Working Party on Discipline in Schools in Northern Ireland*. HMSO, Belfast.

Dierenfield, R.B. (1982). *Classroom Disruption in English Comprehensive Schools. Macalester College, St Paul, Minnesota.*

Eggleston, J., Dunn, D. and Anjali, M. (1986) *Education for Some.* Trentham Books.

Frude, N. and Gault, G. (eds.) (1984). *Disruptive Behaviour in Schools.* John Wiley.

Galton, M. and Wilcocks. (1983). *Moving from the Primary Classroom.* Routledge and Kegan Paul.

HMI (1978). *Behavioural Units. A survey of special units for pupils with behavioural problems.* H.M.S.O. London.

Kelly, E. and Cohn, T. (1988). *Racism in Schools: new research evidence.* Trentham Books.

Lowenstein, L.F. (1975). *Violent and Disruptive Behaviour in Schools.* N.A.S., Hemel Hempstead.

Measor, L. and Woods, P. (1984). *Changing Schools.* Open University Press.

Newson, J. and Newson, E. (1984). Parents Perspectives on Children's Behaviour in School. In N. Frude and G. Gault (eds.), *Disruptive Behaviour in Schools.* John Wiley.

Olweus, D. (1984). Aggressors and their Victims: Bullying at School. In N. Frude and G. Gault (eds.), *Disruptive Behaviour in Schools.* John Wiley.

Swann Report, (1985). *Education for All.* H.M.S.O., 1985.

Tattum, D.P. (1982). *Disruptive Pupils in Schools and Units.* John Wiley.

West, D.J. and Farrington, D.P. (1973). *Who Becomes Delinquent?* Heinemann.

Youngman, M.B., and Lunzer, E. (1977). *Adjustment to Secondary School.* University of Nottingham School of Education.

BULLYING IN SCHOOLS

Chapter 2
Bullying: The Scandinavian Research Tradition
Erling Roland

For several years, research activity concerning bullying in school was restricted to the Scandinavian countries and Finland. Fortunately, there now seems to be a rapidly growing interest in the bullying problem in Western Europe, the USA, Japan, and other countries as well.

The Scandinavian research tradition can be dated back to 1969 when a Swedish doctor of medicine wrote a semi-popular article about a phenomenon which he named 'mobbing' (Heinemann, 1969). He borrowed this term from Konrad Lorenz who had used it to describe a particular behaviour which occurred among animals, namely a mass attack directed against a deviant individual. The article was accepted with great interest in Sweden, among both laymen and professionals, and Heinemann was inspired to continue his studies. The result was a book published in 1972 in Sweden and the following year in Norway. Heinemann based his conclusions on his own observations in Swedish school-grounds. He describes the phenomenon and proposes some theoretical suggestions. Mainly, Heinemann sees mobbing as somewhat uncontrolled group violence directed against an individual who has disturbed the group's ordinary activities. When the violent attack is completed, the group members who have carried out these acts of violence, will again resume their roles as normal, ordinary individuals (Heinemann, 1973).

Since then, several research programs on mobbing have been conducted in Scandinavia (Olweus, 1974, 1978, 1985; Pikas, 1976, 1987; Mykletun, 1979; Roland, 1980, 1983, 1987; Bjorkqvist et al., 1982; Lagerspetz et al., 1982; Befring, 1983; Olweus & Roland, 1983; Aarland, 1986).

A Common Definition

Heinemann (1969, 1973) understood mobbing as a rather accidental mass activity. This is not the common opinion today. On the contrary, the stability aspect is strongly emphasized. The following definition, which I believe can be regarded as generally accepted in Scandinavia today, demonstrates this clearly:

Bullying is longstanding violence, physical or psychological, conducted by an individual or a group and directed against an individual who is not able to defend himself in the actual situation.

This definition states that bullying is a fairly stable kind of interaction between a violent agent and a somewhat helpless victim. This clearly excludes the conflict aspect, and thus we maintain that mobbing is not a give-and-take activity, but rather an unbalanced, one-way form of violence. The victim is forced into this situation, he suffers from it and tries desperately to avoid it or escape from it.

The terms 'physical' and 'psychological' indicate that the violent means may be of different natures. There is physical bullying, such as kicking, pushing or beating the victim. The psychological means are generally of two kinds: teasing or exclusion. Teasing is to humiliate the victim through the use of words or gestures. Exclusion is to make the victim believe that he is allowed to join the group and then to reject him (Roland 1987). These various forms of bullying are used in different degrees and depending on whether the bullies are boys or girls. This I shall return to later.

The Size of the Problem

To most Scandinavian people, who I believe tend to look at our small nations as a peaceful corner of the world, it has been surprising and provocative to learn that the bullying problem in school is certainly quite serious.

Of course, the findings of different investigations do vary, due to the methods of research and the definitions used, and certainly also due to real differences among the schools studies. However, it is widely accepted that *at least 5%* of the children in primary and secondary schools (ages 7-16) are victims of bullying (Olweus, 1978, 85; Mykletun, 1979; Roland, 1980, 87; Bjorkqvist et al., 1982; Lagerspetz et al., 1982). For Denmark, Finalnd, Sweden and Norway as a whole, one must face up to the fact that about 200,000 children suffer frequent and longstanding victimization.

Similarly, it is estimated that about the same number of pupils are involved as bullies (Olweus, 1978, 85; Mykletun, 1979; Roland, 1980, 87; Bjorkqvist et al., 1982; Lagerspetz et al., 1982). There should be no doubt then that a large number of pupils are involved in bullying as either victims or bullies in Scandinavian schools today.

As a general rule, the positions as bullies and victims are occupied by different pupils. However, one has found that about 20% of the victims also act as bullies (Olweus, 1978; Mykletun, 1979; Roland, 1980, 87). Here it is important to note that the bullying these children carry out is nearly always directed against pupils other than their own offenders (Roland, 1987).

Boys and Girls

It is a stable finding that there are about twice as many victims among boys than among girls, and the figures for bullies are about three times as high for boys as for girls (Roland, 1980; Olweus, 1985). In my opinion, these figures are misleading. The referred findings are all based on the pupils' own answers to questionnaires, and there are reasons to believe that girls, more than boys, are unwilling to answer truthfully to questions concerning their own involvement in violent interactions (Tieger, 1980; Roland, 1987). Findings from an exhaustive interview study among 300 pupils in grades four to six (10-12 years of age), indicate that girls are involved almost as much as boys, both as victims and as bullies. However, the means used by the two sexes are in many respects different.

Both boys and girls use teasing as a means of bullying. In addition, boys use physical means whereas girls use exclusion. Predominantly, boys bully other boys.

They do, however, to a significant degree, also bully girls. The children who are the victims of boys' bullying can be classmates or other pupils at the school. The pattern found for girls differs from this; most commonly, girls bully other girls in their own class (Roland, 1987).

Age

From several investigations, one can estimate with great certainty that the percentage of victims decreases with an increase of age (Roland, 1980; Olweus & Roland, 1983; Olweus, 1985). This is the case for both sexes.

This tendency is not shared by the bullies. Looking at figures representing bullies, one finds that the percentages are quite similar at different age levels, but the number of girl-bullies does decline slightly with increasing age (Roland, 1980; Olweus, 1985).

Physical appearance

Surprisingly, physical appearance does not seem to be as important as commonly supposed.

In a study comprising only boys, Dan Olweus (1978) asked the teachers to evaluate all their pupils' physical characteristics. He found that the victims among these boys were physically weaker than their peers (see also Roland, 1987). Aside from this, the victims did not seem to have more irregular traits than their classmates (Olweus, 1978).

The point made by Olweus, and with which I agree, is that almost everyone has one or more physical traits which make them stand out from others. When a pupil is known to be a victim of bullying, one tends to think that this is because of his/her red hair, long nose, glasses or whatever. One forgets that other pupils who are not bullied also have similar physical irregularities.

By this I do not mean that physical appearance is unimportant. My point is that the pupils' looks have so far often been overestimated as the sole reason for being bullied.

For girls, physical strength seems to be quite irrelevant (Roland, 1987), but unfortunately, the importance of other physical traits has not been investigated for girls.

In the Olweus study (1978), it was also found that the bullies were quite normal as concerns physical appearance except for physical strength: the boy bullies were stronger than their male peers. (See also same results in Roland, 1987). This was not the case for girls. In fact, the girl bullies were slightly weaker than their female classmates (Roland, 1987). The significance of physical appearance was not investigated for girls.

My conclusion is that physical traits, except for physical strength, seem to be overestimated as 'reasons' for why pupils are victims or bullies. This is at least true for boys. One should, however, be careful to say that this conclusion has been drawn on a general level. There may well be individual cases that can be regarded as exceptions.

Does this mean that individual factors are unimportant as explanations of bullying?

Psychological Traits

It has been demonstrated repeatedly that some psychological traits are connected with positions as bully or victim.

Victims earn significantly lower school grades than pupils not involved in bullying, and they are also less intelligent (Olweus, 1978; Roland, 1980, 87). This holds true for both boys and girls. The boy bullies are also below average on school grades and intelligence (Olweus, 1978; Roland, 1980, 87), but this is not the case for girl bullies. Quite the contrary, these girls receive better grades than those not involved in bullying and they are also slightly more intelligent (Roland, 1980, 87).

Victims of both sexes are very low on self-esteem (Olweus, 1978; Mykletun, 1979; Bjorkqvist et al., 1982). This may, of course, be seen as a reason for being bullied, but a low self-esteem is probably also, at least to some degree, a result of humiliating experiences on the part of the victim. In fact, some of the victims seem to start thinking that they 'deserve it' (Roland, 1980).

Counteracting Bullying

It is widely recognized in our Scandinavian society that victims of bullying are in a highly humiliating position, and today there is much concern about this among parents, teachers and professionals. I think that this public and professional interest is mainly due to the research programmes, the results of which have been disseminated through books, articles, periodicals and other mass media. These well-known programmes and approaches have served as models for many small-scale and local investigations which have focused on the problem in particular schools or local communities.

I believe that this research has been a predisposition for the public interest and concern about bullying in Scandinavia. There is of course always a private interest in such matters of violence; the parents of the child may be deeply worried, and likewise the teachers. However, they constitute only thousands of isolated islands of concern in a society. They have no suitable concepts and no network for communication.

I also believe that this research, by its creation of public and professional concern, is necessary in order to get wheels moving so as to provide help in combating these problems.

Private concern elicits private action — for better or for worse. Public concern, on the other hand, creates a market, and there has obviously been a market created in Scandinavia for management of behaviour literature.

Olweus offered some suggestions to counteract bullying in his first research report (1974 — in English 1978). Pikas (1976) wrote the first book about management. This book has been greatly extended and revised (1987). Also Roland (1983), and Aarland (1986) have published books about management. Some of these have been translated and spread throughout Scandinavia (Olewus, 1974;

Pikas, 1976; Roland, 1983). Hundreds of courses for parents, teachers, school psychologists and others have been arranged and many colleges and universities run seminars for their students about bullying in school.

Thus, I am quite certain that bullying, like other similar underworld phenomena needs to be focused on by research programmes to gain public and professional concern. The process can be illustrated as follows:

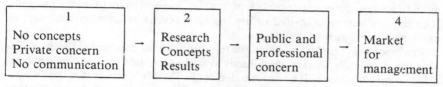

This process, when started by research, will of course not end up at a final stage four. Instead, stages two, three and four will constitute an integrated system of circles activating each other. This process, going on in Scandinavia since about 1970, was certainly a predisposition for the Norwegian campaign against bullying in 1983.

The Norwegian Campaign Against Bullying

Two young people took their own lives in late 1982, and the local social service concluded that longstanding victimization was the reason for both these tragic incidents of suicide. This was, of course, a shock to everyone, and especially to the school authorities.

In my opinion, these two incidents were the direct reason for the Norwegian Campaign Against Bullying. Still, the campaign would have been unthinkable without the general concern about bullying already prevalent in Norway.

The bullying problem was discussed at the top level of the Ministry of Education, and in February 1983, about 15 people were invited by the Minister to attend a meeting at the Department. The Minister stated his deep concern about the problem, and all of those present, mostly school politicians and professionals, recommended that something must be done. The Minister concluded that the Department should take action in this case. A working party was to be set up and would be led by the Deputy Minister of Education.

The meeting and the statement made by the Minister received good coverage by the Norwegian Broadcasting Services and by the press.

The working party, of which I was a member, was set up about a month later. We decided that a nationwide campaign against bullying in the primary and secondary schools should be conducted, and that the start of this was to be 1st October, 1983.

The Working Party

It was agreed that a video film about bullying should be made and also a 'package' of written material. This package, which was made up of one article for the teachers, a brochure for the parents and some other material, was to be distributed to all of the 3500 primary and secondary schools in Norway. The article (Olweus & Roland, 1983) was published in about 20,000 copies, and the brochures for the parents in about 600,000 copies. This was all financed by the Department. The video film had to be bought by the schools, but the Department subsidized it.

It was also agreed that a questionnaire should be answered by all the pupils about one week before the Campaign was to start. The intentions were twofold; both to see how serious the problem of bullying was and to focus on the problem. The schools were also invited to use the local results as an integrated part of their own work against bullying.

Professor Dan Olweus was given the responsibility for conducting the investigation and he was allocated research funds to analyse the data representing a nationwide sample of schools. It was also stated by the Deputy Minister that the Department would try to provide funds for a follow-up investigation to see whether the campaign had had any effect.

It should be noted that the Norwegian Government was reorganized in the early summer of 1983. The first three meetings of the working party were led by the Deputy Minister representing the Conservative party, but the meetings succeeding the reorganization were led by the Deputy Minister representing the Christian Party who, as the new Minister, had decided to continue this work.

Stage I: The Nationwide Survey

Shortly before the 'package' was released, a nationwide investigation into bullying in grades 2-9 was conducted by Olweus. All schools were invited to participate, which meant a total of about 600,000 pupils. From these, a representative sample of about 80,000 pupils was drawn for analysis. The graphs below show some of the main tendencies found:

Table 1: Percentages of pupils victimized at school (Autumn 1983) 'now and then or more often'. Boys and girls (Olweus, 1988)

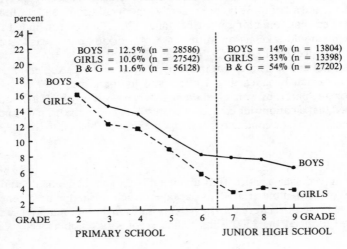

Nearly 10% of the pupils stated that they had been bullied that autumn. This is a remarkably high figure for a questionnaire investigation, especially when considering that the period of time 'this autumn' represented less than two months of the new school year. One should however note that Olweus uses the criterion 'now and then or more often', and in the questionnaire it explains that 'more often' means at least once a week. If the more conventional criterion 'once a week or more often' had been used, the figures would most probably have been less dramatic.

The figures for bullies are shown in Table 2.

Table 2: Percentages of pupils who have bullied other children at school (Autumn 1983) 'now and then or more often'. Boys and girls (Olweus, 1988)

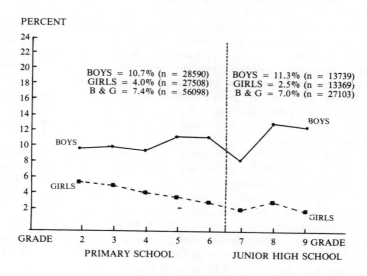

Using this 'now and then or more often' criterion, slightly above 7% of the children asked stated that they had bullied other pupils that autumn. Many more boys than girls reported this, which is a common finding when questionnaires are used.

Mainly, this large scale investigation confirmed what had been found in previous studies, also in relation to age tendencies. It became obvious that there was work to be done!

Stage 2: The National Campaign

Following the national survey the 'action' part of the Campaign was implemented. In October 1983 the video film and 'package' of materials had been prepared ready for distribution to teachers and parents. To launch the Campaign a press concerence was called by the Deputy Minister and working party. Nearly

30 journalists from Norwegian TV and radio, the press and several journals were present. Some sequences from the video film and an interview with the Deputy Minister were shown on the evening news. Interviews with other members of the working party were broadcast on several radio programmes and most of the newspapers in Norway covered the news. Also, the teachers' journals published articles about the Campaign. This was all done in a very positive fashion and because of all the attention it received, the Campaign was well known all over Norway.

Stage 3: The Janus Project[1]

The Department of Education generously provided funds for a follow-up project, which was called the Janus Project. The Project has two main aims. The first is to investigate the effect of the Campaign against bullying of 1983. Some of the results are reported here. The second aim is to study the connections between leadership in the classroom, social structures in the class and different behaviour problems (i.e. bullying, use of stimulants, disruption, truancy and school phobia, stealing and criminal behaviour) among the pupils. Also we will study the connections between these behaviour problems. It was decided that this study should be carried out in Rogaland, a rather large county along the south-west coast of Norway. Nearly 10% of the Norwegian population live in Rogaland, and the county was regarded as fairly representative of the Norwegian community with reference to both the structure of urbanization and the school system and population.

The investigation was to comprise the same 40 schools that had participated in 1983. Three schools preferred not to participate again, and thus we were left with 37 schools, both primary (grades 1-6) and secondary (grades 7-9). All of nearly 7,000 pupils answered the same questionnaire as was used in 1983. We also made more exhaustive questionnaires which were used in 70 classes, in addition to the inventory on bullying, which will be used in our study of various behaviour problems. The 70 teachers of these pupils were interviewed as were the headteachers of the 37 schools and the district school administrators. The investigation was carried out in October 1986, three years after the first one.

Preliminary results

According to the interviews with the headteachers and teachers, *nearly all of the 37 schools* had used some part of the 'package' or the film to counteract bullying.

If we believe that this is representative of Norway, this means that a large majority of the 3,500 schools did use some part of the material distributed or the video in their work. Thus, we can conclude that the campaign did have an effect in the sense that it was in fact used.

However, we are also aware that the degree of use varied greatly from one school to another.

When it comes to the amount of bullying, I have plotted in the percentages of boys being bullied in 1983 and 1986 in the table below:

Table 3: Percentages of boys being victimized in 1983 and 1986 'once a week or more often', grades 4-9 (10-16 years)

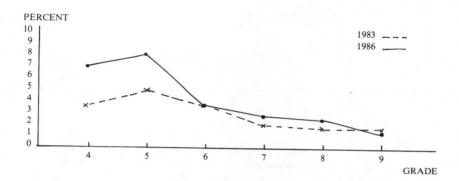

We have chosen not to include the 'now and then' category, and have also disregarded grades 2 and 3, because of information received from teachers who had administered the questionnaires in those grades. They maintained that the pupils had difficulties understanding the questions. This can also be seen in the pattern of answers in this age group.

The curve shows that the percentage of victims among boys has increased from 1983 to 1986. This is particularly the case for grades 4 and 5 (ages 10-11).

Table 4: Percentage of girls being victimized in 1983 and 1986 'once a week or more often', grades 4-9 (10-16 years)

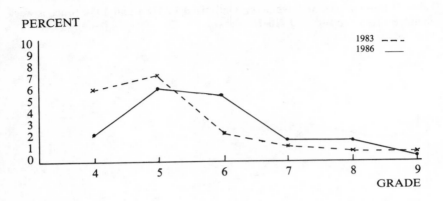

Here one can see that, whereas the percentage of boys being victimized had increased over the 3-year span, the percentage has in fact decreased for girls. Also, whereas the increase was most evident for grades 4 and 5 among boys, the decrease is most evident in the 4th grade among girls.

Table 5 below shows the percentages of boy bullies at the different grade levels. These curves, representing 1983 and 1986, illustrate that the oldest boys at each school type are the ones who admit to being most active as aggressors.

Table 5: Percentage of boy bullies in 1983 and 1986 'once a week or more often', grades 4-9

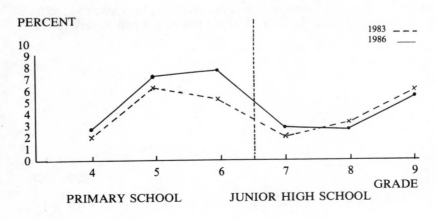

Here too, one sees that there has been an increase in boys' involvement in bullying in the role as aggressor. From the next table presented, we can read that girls admit to bullying about as much in 1983 as in 1986. The finding is quite stable.

Table 6: Percentage of girl bullies in 1983 and 1986 'once a week or more often', grades 4-9

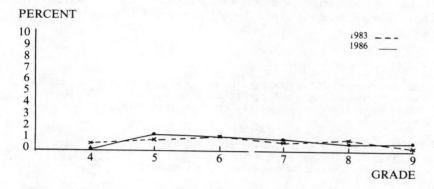

Preliminary conclusions

In general, one has to conclude that the problem of bullying has increased slightly in Rogaland from 1983 to 1986. This is not a satisfactory outcome and absolutely not what was hoped for when the campaign was initiated. Perhaps the campaign had no effect, or even worse, maybe the campaign exacerbated the problem.

This final observation is too depressing to consider, if, in fact, it was the case; but a closer examination of the data demonstrates that when one correlates the *differences* between the results of 1983 and those of 1986 with the corresponding involvement level in the campaign at each school, that is, how much they used the package and film, one finds a small but steady decreasing level of bullying at high-involvement schools and an increasing tendency in low-involvement schools. Though the tendency is not very strong, it is stable for a number of different indicators of bullying. Therefore, we concluded that where a school adopted an active programme against bullying it was measurably successful, but in other schools the problem of bullying has worsened. In other words, in schools which express public concern and have a policy and programme of work to counter bullying there is a desired effect, but this has to be seen against wider social changes.

It is expected that we will be in a better position to attempt an explanation of the changes in the incidence in bullying in Rogaland when our remaining analyses are completed. We have access to interesting data, both about changes in the local community and in the schools themselves during this 3 year period, and the results will be reported at a later date.

Finally, we look forward to further work in part two of the Janus Project. This is about teachers' different styles of leadership, social structures in the classroom and various behavioural problems. Hopefully these studies will result in new knowledge about the whole complex of behaviour problems in schools and in the ways management strategies are connected with them. It is our belief that this will be a fruitful way to gain deeper understanding of bullying behaviour in particular.

Note

1. *The Janus Project*
   The research leader is Erling Roland and the research assistants are Peter Steen and Bjorg Lauvvik (the first half of the project period) and Elaine Munthe (the whole 3-year project period 1986-1988). Address: Stavanger College of Education, POB 2521, 4004 Stavanger, Norway.

References

Aarland, S.O., 1986. *Alene eller sammen.* Oslo: Gyldendal.

Befring, E., 1983. *Skole-og atferdsproblem i omsorgspedagogisk perspektiv.* Oslo: Universitetsforlaget.

Bjorkqvist, K., Ekman, K. and Lagerspetz, K., 1982. Bullies and victims: Their ego picture, ideal ego picture and normative ego picture. *Scandinavian Journal of Psychology* 23, 307-313.

Heinemann, P.P., 1969. *Apartheid.* Liberal Debatt no. 2.

Heinemann, P.P., 1973. *Mobbing. Gruppevold blant barn og vokane.* Oslo: Gyldendal.

Lagerspetz, K.M., Bjorkqvist, K., Berts, M. and King, E., 1982. Group aggression among school children in three schools. *Scandinavian Journal of Psychology* 23, 45-52.

Mykletun, R.J., 1979. *Plaging i skolen.* Stavanger: Rogalandsforskning.

Olweus, D., 1974. *Hakkekyllinger og skoleboller. Forskning om skolemobbing.* Oslo: Cappelen.

Olweus, D., 1978. *Aggression in the schools: Bullies and whipping boys.* Washington D.C.: Hemisphere Press.

Olweus, D., 1985. *80,000 elever innblandet i mobbing.* Norak Skoleblad no. 2.

Olweus, D., 1988. Bully/Victim problems among schoolchildren. To appear in J.P. Myklebust and R. Ommundsen (eds.) *Psykologprofesjonen mot ar 2000: Arbeidsliv, internasjonalisering og utdannelse.* (in press).

Olweus, D. and Roland, E., 1983. *Mobbing — Bakgrunn og tiltak.* Oslo: Kirke-og under visningsdepartementet.

Pikas, A., 1976. *Slik stopper vi mobbing.* Oslo: Gyldendal.

Pikas, A., 1987. *Sa bekampar vi mobbning i skolan.* Uppsala: AMA Dataservice.

Roland, E., 1980. *Terror i skolen.* Stavanger: Rogalandsforskning.

Roland, E., 1983. *Strategi mot mobbing.* Stavanger: Universitetsforlaget.

Roland, E., 1987. *Kjonnstypisk mobbing.* Stavanger Laererhogskole.

Chapter 3
Bullying in the Infant School
Maurice Chazan

The beginnings of bullying in young children

It is difficult to state precisely when bullying begins in young children, especially when the term is used in the sense of deliberate intent to cause physical injury or distress by psychological means (teasing, mocking or taunting), or to extort something from others (Crabtree, 1981). Maccoby (1980) emphasises that a child needs to have reached an appropriate level of cognitive development, involving an understanding of the self and of the feelings of others, in order to be capable of carrying out an intentionally hurtful act. However, as Maccoby further points out, parents begin to teach their children at an early age that their actions may cause distress, and most young children witness deliberate acts of aggression in their own families or on the television screen. It is not surprising, therefore, that by the time they are of nursery school age, children know many ways in which they can hurt others.

That some nursery school children resort to behaviour which is tantamount to bullying has been shown by Manning et al. (1978), who found cases of 'harassment' and 'game hostility' in their sample of three to five year-olds. 'Harassment' is defined as unprovoked aggression, at least in the immediate situation, directed at a person, often the same one repeatedly. The aggressor, who is 'rewarded' by the victim's reaction, indulges in physical harassment (e.g. sudden gripping, or ruffling hair), teasing (e.g. interfering with activities, taunting) or threats (e.g. physical or verbal threats of violence or hostility — 'I'll tell the teacher' or 'I won't invite you to my birthday party'). 'Game hostility' includes very rough and intimidating behaviour, usually in the course of a fantasy game. In a follow-up study, Manning and her colleagues found that patterns of aggressive behaviour shown by individuals in the nursery school tended to be still present at 7 to 8 years of age.

Patterson et al. (1967), in their study of three and four year-old nursery school children in the USA, also observed many examples of aggression which involved a victim giving up a toy to the aggressor, running away or crying. If the aggressor felt 'rewarded' as a result of his/her behaviour, he or she was much more likely to repeat the attack on the same victim. Already at this stage some children were learning that aggressive acts could have a successful outcome.

Prevalence and nature of bullying in the infant school

Most infant school teachers readily identify one or two children in their class as presenting aggressive behaviour of some kind which marks them out for special attention. Surveys have indicated that the prevalence of aggressive or anti-social behaviour in five to seven year-olds ranges from about 5 to over 20 per cent: estimates vary according to the location and nature of the sample, the criteria used for ratings of aggressiveness and whether teachers, parents or others make

33

the judgements (see Laing and Chazan, 1986). Only a minority of teachers, however, seem to have experience of bullying in the infant school. When a sample of 40 infant school teachers in South Wales was asked to provide examples of incidents of bullying which they had come across for the purpose of illustrating this chapter, two-thirds were unable to do so.

There is little survey data on the prevalence of bullying in infant schools, but Yule (1970), in a study of the total infant school intake on the Isle of Wight at the beginning of the autumn term (N = 435), asked both scale teachers and parents to complete the Rutter Child Behaviour Scale (Infants) during the children's first term at school. The Rutter Scale contains the item 'bullies other children'. In the sample of boys (N = 209), the teachers rated this statement as 'certainly applies' in 1.4 per cent, and as 'applies somewhat' in a further 8.1 per cent of cases. In the sample of girls (N = 226), the teachers endorsed 'certainly applies' in 1 per cent, and 'applies somewhat' in 6.6 per cent of cases. As would be expected from previous studies of aggression in young children (see for example, Chazan and Jackson, 1971, 1974; Hughes et al., 1979), rather more boys than girls were seen as presenting bullying behaviour. The parents' survey showed a lower prevalence of bullying at home than in school, the parents responding that the item 'bullies other children' applied to 0.5 per cent of the samples of both boys and girls, with 'applies somewhat' being ticked in the case of 7.3 per cent of the boys, and 4.4 per cent of the girls.

Manning et al. (1978) found that children who were hostile at school were not necessarily so at home, and the studies by John and Elizabeth Newson (1968, 1978, 1984) suggest that, not unexpectedly, parents were more ready to produce examples of their children being victimised by other children than to admit bullying on the part of their own children. In a more recent survey by Osborn et al. (1984), who administered a modification of the Rutter Child Behaviour Scale (retaining the item on bullying) to the mothers of a large national sample of 5 year-olds at home (N = 13,135), the item was rated as 'certainly applies' in 1.5 per cent, and as 'applies somewhat' in 13.9 per cent of cases.

Few books covering development during the infant school years include any detailed discussion of bullying at this stage, if the topic is even mentioned. However, Webb (1969) refers to gangs of six and seven year-olds who cause harm, emotional and/or physical, to younger or less aggressive children. Among children whose case histories are outlined by Webb, D. (aged 6) is described as the leader of a little gang, who terrorised younger children on the way to and from school; and S. (aged 7) also bullied small children out of school — on one occasion being caught 'with his little gang watching in admiration, as he removed a cap from a passing five year-old, kicked it into a garden, and threatened to twist the child's arm if he told anyone' (Webb, 1969, p.46).

Mitchell (1973), while stating that 'no young child of five can be called a bully', acknowledges that bullying may begin in the infant school: for example, a child with a strong personality may dominate a weaker one, perhaps a so-called friend or frequent companion. John and Elizabeth Newson (1978), in their study of seven year-olds in their home environment, although not suggesting that a large

34

number of children of this age are bullies, refer to the pleasure which some children derive from bullying, and to the cunning with which they can keep it secret long enough to make a victim's life a misery.

The following examples, given by the South Wales teachers, illustrate the nature of bullying in the infant school:

Case 1. 'A. is a five-year old girl in a reception class who is very big for her age. She consistently picks on children who are much smaller than herself. She always wants to be in the forefront: one particular incident was when she pushed a much smaller child out of the way so that she fell to the floor, just in order that she might be first in the line.'

Case 2. 'The incident involved two boys, one aged 7 and one aged 5. In the school playground the teacher observed the older boy with his hands cupped full of crisps. As the crisps were not in a bag, the teacher asked where he had got them. The boy replied, " — gave them to me". When the younger child was asked if he gave them to the older boy, he said they had been taken from him.'

Case 3. 'M. is a seven year-old boy. His bullying behaviour first became apparent when a girl in a parallel class said that she was being threatened by M. Words used were, "He's going to beat me up, Miss". She became terrified and was afraid to go out into the playground . . . After action was taken, the bullying ceased in the case of this girl, but recurred with another girl in M's own class.'

Case 4. 'C. was a tall, well-built boy aged 7 years in the top class of an infant school, who victimised anyone weaker than himself. He pushed, kicked, punched and hit other children, both inside the classroom and in the playground, and at any time of the day, including before school commenced. C's apparent intention was personal gain, to acquire the possessions of other children, such as crisps, balls, toys or sweets.'

The victims

Even less attention has been paid by researchers to the victims of bullying in the early years at school than to the bullies themselves; yet the victims may well be in need of help in adjusting to school life and in participating in the activities of the peer group. Studies of victims of bullying in older age groups suggest that most of these children are weak, passive and socially ineffective; anxious, insecure and lacking in self-confidence; and unpopular with other children (Olweus, 1984; Stephenson and Smith, 1987). They may come home from school without some of their belongings, or show some deterioration in their work, or even be afraid to go to school at all (Crabtree, 1981; Mortimore *et al.,* 1983). A small number of victims may be assertive and provocative, seeming to invite aggressive acts against them (Olweus, 1984; Stephenson and Smith, 1987) Obvious physical stigmata may result in teasing and taunting, as the following case presented by an infant school teacher graphically illustrates:

Case 5. 'B is a seven year-old boy. His right hand had been badly burnt as a baby, and the skin from his forearm was grafted in a large flap between thumb and index finger. The flap was overlarge to allow growth and to avoid further plastic surgery. B. is dark-haired and the flap of skin has dark hairs growing from it. The boy is a quiet, timid boy, who was tormented in the school yard by some boys in his class. Taunts such as "hairy hands" were made. His sister who was in the reception class, told their mother, who had not been able to understand why her son was so tearful and disliked school. She understood at last and came to see the teacher. The boy B. had brought sweets and other things, and tried to bribe other boys to be his friends.'

After action had been taken by the teacher, the incidents were not repeated, but in the first-year junior class to which B. went from the infant school, he was again bullied. 'He presents as being one of life's victims.'

Apart from those with stigmata of the kind described above, children perceived by others in their class as different in any marked way, for example in appearance, manners or speech, are at risk of victimization. Adults, too, do not find it easy to avoid showing excessive liking for a particularly attractive child, or dislike of one who is unappealing or difficult to control. Nevertheless, it is important for teachers to be aware that their own attitudes to individual pupils, even if covertly rather than openly expressed, could contribute to a child being unpopular in the group and regarded as a target for attack by some of its members.

Assessment
General principles. The general principles which apply to the assessment of young children with emotional or behavioural problems hold good for the assessment of both bullies and their victims. In particular, it is important

a)   to ascertain, as precisely as possible, both the nature and the context of the difficulties presented;
b)   to draw up a profile of the several aspects of the child's development, including strengths as well as weaknesses observed over a period of time;
c)   to link assessment closely to intervention;
d)   to involve the parents, getting to know something of the child's home background; and
e)   to enlist, if necessary, the aid of the support services (e.g. the schools psychological service).

(See Chazan et al., 1983, Section 3, and 1987, Chapter 7, for a more detailed discussion of the assessment of behaviour difficulties in children up to 8 years of age.)

Sociometric techniques. Since both bullies and their victims are usually far from well integrated into the peer group (Hartup, 1983), a teacher might find a simple sociometric chart of the class as a whole useful, particularly after its members have had sufficient time to get to know one another. Such a chart or sociogram will help the teacher to see who are the isolates within the class as well as what sub-groups exist. Fontana (1981) observes that the teacher can do much to prevent vulnerable individuals from becoming isolates by ensuring that children are not always left to define their own social environments within the class, though he cautions that this needs to be done with sensitivity.

Cohen (1976) points out that very little use has been made of sociometric techniques in nursery or infant classes, even though it could be argued that the peer group is particularly important in the social development of young children. Cohen gives details of the application and scoring of two methods of obtaining sociometric data from younger pupils:

a) through asking the children individually to name children in their group or class whom they 'like best to play with' and whom they 'don't like to play with', and then 'Anyone else? Anyone else?' In this way, an attempt is made to obtain three choices and three rejections from each child (Dunnington, 1957).

b) through the use of photographs of the members of the class, using questions such as:
Who do you like to play with in the playground?
Who do you like to play with in school?
Who do you like to sit next to during story-time?
(McCandless and Marshall, 1957).

The use of positive questions only may be preferred to a method which involves questions calling for rejections.

Explanations of bullying in young children

Various hypotheses have been put forward to explain bullying in young children. This is not surprising, since bullies may be big, tough and strong or they may be weak and usually timid children seeking to assert themselves by aggressive acts. They may be complete isolates, with a low status in the peer group, or they may be well-integrated members of a sub-group or gang. It is generally agreed, however, that both learning and inborn temperamental tendencies are involved in the development of aggression (Maccoby, 1980). Bates (1980), for example, asserts that the development of severe behaviour problems may require a combination of variables such as a difficult temperament in addition to adverse parental attitudes and practices. Even Olweus (1984), who, on the basis of research mainly confined to boys aged 13 to 15 in Sweden, favours a personality explanation of bullying, acknowledges the role of early child rearing practices in the genesis of bullying. Although Olweus finds it difficult to explain the behaviour of highly aggressive bullies as a consequence of their being exposed to unusually favourable situations or conditions in the school setting, his studies indicate that important variables, in addition to temperament, were the mother's negativism (indifference and lack of involvement) and tolerance of aggressive behaviour during the first four or five years of life.

A number of other studies have emphasised the part played by the child's family background in providing models of aggression or in creating emotional disturbance in the child which might lead to maladaptive behaviour. For example, Webb

(1969) gives examples of infant school bullies who were exposed to parental inconsistency, rejection or aggression at home. Manning et al. (1978) found that young children who harassed others in school tended to have overcontrolling and dominating home environments. Mitchell (1973) draws attention to the considerable number of young children who receive and witness violence at home, to such an extent that they can come to regard violence as normal behaviour. According to Lefkowitz et al. (1977), violence seen on television may also have an effect on the development of aggression, especially in boys. Stevenson-Hinde and Simpson (1982) point out that behavioural characteristics become more tightly linked to environmental influences as the child gets older. However, they caution that we must not think in terms of direct effects of home experiences on school behaviour but rather of these experiences producing both temporary responses and longer-term predispositions in the child that affect behaviour in school (Stevenson-Hinde et al., 1986). It is possible too, that even where the home background is conducive to aggressiveness, the opportunity to interact with other children at the pre-school stage reduces the risk of a child indulging in domineering behaviour in the infant school.

Case 4, described above, highlights a combination of adverse home background factors:

(i)   both parents had attended Borstal for violent behaviour;
(ii) the parents were violent towards their children;
(iii) the children had been in a series of foster-homes; and
(iv) the child C's behaviour was markedly worse after visits to see his mother, who had only limited access to him.

School factors related to aggressiveness have not received a great deal of attention in the case of 5 to 7 year-olds, who in general enjoy a very congenial environment at school. However, the possible effects of teachers' attitudes to individual pupils have already been mentioned. King (1978) too found differences between infant schools in the general behaviour of their pupils. In one school, as King reports, '. . . both the teacher and I could see from time to time some children, covertly or openly, pinch, push, punch, bite, scratch, kick, spit and shout at other children . . .' (p.88). In other schools, no such problems were observed. Such differences may be related, at least in part, to the catchment area served by a particular school rather than to the way in which schools and classes are managed. Even so, an over-dominant or weak teacher, or poor supervision in the playground, may encourage bullying (Crabtree, 1981). Patterson et al. (1967), in their studies of nursery school children in the USA, observed that the nature of the programme of activities arranged by individual teachers and the way in which teachers exercised control over individual children had considerable bearing on the amount of aggression that occurred within a group.

Intervention

When bullying in school is identified, immediate action is called for, in the interests of all concerned. However, longer-term measures should also be considered, as both bullies and victims are likely to benefit from special help with their development and adjustment over a substantial period of time.

Immediate action. Immediate action to deal with bullying in the infant school usually involves (Webb, 1969; Crabtree, 1981; Manning and Sluckin, 1984):

a) the teacher talking calmly to the bully, making it clear that bullying is unacceptable;
b) reassuring the victim that action is being taken to stop the bullying;
c) inviting the co-operation of the parents;
d) increasing supervision by adults in school and playground, and ensuring that the children involved are escorted to and from school;
e) giving constructive tasks to the bully, while possibly removing some privileges from him/her;
f) breaking up bullying gangs; and
g) using members of the class to support the victim.

Action along these lines is illustrated by the examples provided by the infant school teachers:

In *Case 2* (see above), the teacher made the 7 year old-boy who had forcibly taken some crisps from a younger child return the crisps and reprimanded him. He was told that he could not take things from other children just because he did not have any himself. This was in itself an incident that might be thought hardly worth mentioning, but the prompt action by the teacher might well have served to prevent the escalation of bullying in this case.

In *Case 3* (see above), the boy M. was spoken to by the victim's class teacher. He was warned that the behaviour was not acceptable and that if it continued, privileges would be withdrawn, e.g. he would remain inside during the class break and be given a specific activity to complete. The victim's mother rang the school expressing her concern and the headteacher also spoke to M. In this case, bullying incidents ceased for the time being after immediate action had been taken, but, in the teacher's words, '. . . What is happening is that the behaviour is being contained within specific situations, but the root cause has not been defined and a positive behavioural approach has not been acted upon in this instance'.

In *Case 4* (see above), the teacher i) withdrew the bully from the group, either to work alone in a small room, or in the headteacher's room; ii) withdrew some special privileges or enjoyable activities, e.g. playing musical instruments or using the computer; and iii) reported the behaviour to the boy's foster parents. The child disliked being withdrawn from the peer group, and so the threat of being withdrawn was sometimes sufficient to modify his behaviour. The reporting of his behaviour also contributed to an improvement, as the boy wanted to be liked and well thought of by his foster parents.

In *Case 5* (described above), the teacher assembled the class (of 6 to 7 year-olds) informally on the carpet, and chatted generally about being brave. The children were asked who had ever remembered being brave. The boy B. (the victim) spoke up: prior to this, he had avoided discussing his hand and would try to hide it. The teacher made a point of saying how good and brave he had been.

This general chat was followed up by a 'private' talk with the bully boys which, after reasoning, explaining and shaming tactics, also included the teacher telling them that she would be 'extremely cross' if they bullied again. Some quicker, gentler boys were appointed special friends to the victim and 'took care' of him: they enjoyed their responsibility.

Longer-term measures. As Olweus (1984) points out, the teacher, by making use of positive resources in a class, has a central position in helping both bullies and victims to find more appropriate forms of reaction patterns. Long-term strategies should be as comprehensive as possible, and may include any combination of the following lines of action, according to the needs of the child and the family (Webb, 1969; Crabtree, 1981; Chazan et al., 1983; Manning and Sluckin, 1984):

(i)   increasing adult participation in play situations to promote appropriate social skills;

(ii)   building up the self-confidence of the victim and, when necessary, the bully as well (see, for example, Burns (1982), Chapter 16);

(iii)   ensuring that the child's learning needs are being met in school;

(iv)   helping parents to adopt more consistent and positive child-rearing practices, or to give more attention to the child's needs. In some cases, this may mean the involvement of the support services;

(v)   teachers examining their own management style to ensure that it does not provide a model of dominating behaviour;

(vi)   employing peer-mediated strategies, e.g. rewarding the whole class for improvements in the behaviour of individuals (Patterson, 1974), or using small groups to promote co-operation. However, Kerr and Nelson (1983) warn against improperly managed group contingency strategies, which may result in the scapegoating and further alienation of an unpopular child;

(vii)   using a problem-solving approach in school to encourage children to modify their behaviour gradually as a result of their own thinking. For examples of this approach with young children, based on Spivack and Shure (1974) and Spivack et al. (1978), see Chazan et al., 1983, pages 177-202. In this approach, the adult, instead of suggesting the most acceptable answer to a problem or explaining why particular actions meet with disapproval, acts as a guide in encouraging children to think up their own ideas of resolving a situation satisfactorily, and to look ahead to possible outcomes. By skilful questioning, bullies may be helped to consider the consequences of their actions, to think about the feelings of others, and themselves to suggest means of gaining satisfaction other than those to which they usually resort. The class as a whole could be helped to a better understanding of words used to describe feelings, such as 'happy', 'sad', 'angry', 'picked-on', 'frightened'.

(viii) planning and implementing behaviour modification programmes, preferably working in collaboration with an educational psychologist. Yule et al. (1984) describe two such programmes carried out, with some success, involving six year-old children in school. Both children indulged in behaviour typical of bullies — pushing, pinching, hitting or kicking some of their classmates. In particular, these programmes focused on rewarding behaviour which was on task or not anti-social rather than on giving attention to inappropriate behaviour. Yule and his colleagues stress that behavioural approaches to classroom problems are flexible, and that ideas for intervention can arise from a rich variety of formulations of classroom problems. However, as they call for considerable changes in the teacher's own behaviour, teachers need support and feedback in carrying out behavioural programmes (see also Walker and Shea, 1976; Axelrod, 1977; Merrett, 1981; Westmacott and Cameron, 1981; Herbert, 1981).

Conclusion

It is tempting for parents and teachers to regard many cases of bullying at the infant school stages as of little real significance. Nevertheless, minor incidents, if not dealt with appropriately, can easily escalate into major ones, and the persistence of behaviour patterns developed in the early years has been demonstrated by longitudinal studies. As already mentioned, Manning et al. (1978) reported the persistence of aggressiveness between three and eight years of age; and Lefkowitz *et al.* (1977) found that aggression at age 8 was the best predictor of aggression at age 19, irrespective of IQ, social class or parental models. Lefkowitz and colleagues also point out that while punishment, when applied with moderation, seems to be effective in reducing aggressiveness, harsh punishment tends to heighten aggression, probably as a result of modelling.

Too little is known about bullies and their victims at the infant school stage, and research to further our knowledge is much needed. However, as this chapter has indicated, teachers have at their disposal a range of positive strategies likely to help young pupils with emotional and behaviour difficulties. The main need is for existing knowledge to be more widely applied in practice.

Acknowledgements

The writer would like to thank Mr Delwyn Tattum (the co-editor of this book) for his help in obtaining case material to illustrate this chapter; all the South Wales infant school teachers who provided accounts of their experience of bullying; and Professor W. Yule, of the Institute of Psychiatry, for permission to quote unpublished data on bullying in five year-olds based on the Isle of Wight surveys.

References

Axelrod, S. (1977) *Behaviour Modification for the Classroom Teacher.* McGraw Hill: New York.
Bates, J.E. (1980) The concept of difficult temperament. *Merrill-Palmer Quarterly,* 26, 299-319.
Burns, R. (1982) *Self-concept, Development and Education,* Holt, Rinehart & Winston.
Chazan, M. and Jackson, S. (1971) Behaviour problems in the infant school. *Journal of Child Psychology and Psychiatry,* 12, 191-210.
Chazan, M. and Jackson, S. (1974). Behaviour problems in the infant school: changes over two years. *Journal of Child Psychology and Psychiatry,* 15, 33-46.

Chazan, M., Laing, A.F., Jones, J., Harper, G.C. and Bolton, J. (1983) *Helping Young Children with Behaviour Difficulties*. Croom Helm.

Chazan, M., Laing, A.F. and Harper, G.C. (1987) *Teaching Five to Eight Year-Olds*. Blackwell.

Cohen, L. (1976) *Educational Research in Classrooms and Schools*. Harper & Row.

Crabtree, T. (1981) *An A-Z of Children's Emotional Problems*. Hamish Hamilton/Elm Tree Books.

Dunnington, M.J. (1957) Behavioural differences of sociometric status groups in a nursery school. *Child Development*, 28, 103-111.

Fontana, D. (1981) *Psychology for Teachers*. British Psychological Society/Macmillan.

Hartup, W.W. (1983) Peer relations. In Mussen, P.H. (ed.) *(Manual of Child Psychology*, 4th ed., Vol. 4 Wiley: New York.

Herbert, M. (1981) *Behavioural Treatment of Problem Children: a practice manual*. Academic Press.

Hughes, M., Pinkerton, G. and Plewis, I. (1979) Children's difficulties on starting infant school. *Journal of Child Psychology and Psychiatry*, 20, 187-196.

Kerr, M.M. and Nelson, C.M. (1983) *Strategies for Managing Behaviour Problems in the Classroom*. Charles E. Merrill: Columbus.

King, R. (1978) *All Things Bright and Beautiful? — a sociological study of infants' classrooms*. John Wiley.

Laing, A.F. and Chazan, M. (1986) The management of aggressive behaviour in young children. In Tattum, D.P. (ed.) *Management of Disruptive Pupil Behaviour in Schools*. John Wiley.

Lefkowitz, M.M., Eron, L.D., Walder, L.O. and Huesmann, L.R. (1977) *Growing Up to be Violent*. Pergamon Press: New York.

McCandless, B.R. and Marshall, H.R. (1957). A picture sociometric technique for pre-school children and its relation to teacher judgements of friendship. *Child Development*, 28, 139-147.

Maccoby, E.E. (1980) *Social Development: psychological growth and the parent-child relationship*. Harcourt Brace Jovanovich: New York.

Manning, M., Heron, J. and Marshall, T. (1978) Styles of hostility and social interactions at nursery, at school and at home: an extended study of children. In Hersov, L.A. and Berger, M. (eds.) *Aggression and Anti-Social Behaviour in Childhood and Adolescence*. Pergamon Press.

Manning, M. and Sluckin, A.M. (1984) The function of aggression in the pre-school and primary-school years. In Frude, N. and Gault, H. (eds.) *Disruptive Behaviour in Schools*. John Wiley.

Merrett, F.E. (1981) Studies in behaviour modification in British educational settings. *Educational Psychology*, 1, 13-38.

Mitchell, C. (1973) *Time for School — a practical guide for parents of young children*. Penguin Education.

Mortimore, P., Davies, J., Varlaam, A. and West, A. (1983) *Behaviour Problems in Schools: an evaluation of support centres*. Croom Helm.

Newson, J. and Newson, E. (1968) *Four Years Old in an Urban Community*. Allen & Unwin.

Newson, J. and Newson, E. (1978). *Seven Years Old in the Home Environment*. Penguin Books.

Newson, J. and Newson, E. (1984) Parents' perspectives on children's behaviour at school. In Frude, N. and Gault, H. (eds.) *Disruptive Behaviour in Schools*. John Wiley.

Olweus, D. (1984) Aggressors and their victims: bullying in school. In Frude, N. and Gault, H. (eds.) *Disruptive Behaviour in Schools*. John Wiley.

Osborn, A.F., Butler, N.R. and Morris, A.C. (1984) *The Social Life of Britain's Five-Year-Olds*. Routledge & Kegan Paul.

Patterson, G.R. (1974) Interventions for boys with multiple conduct problems: multiple settings, treatments and criteria. *Journal of Consulting and Clinical Psychology*, 422, 471-481.

Patterson, G.R., Littman, R.A. and Bricker, W. (1967) *Assertive behaviour in young children: a step towards a theory of aggression*. Monographs of the Society for Research in Child Development, 35, 5.

Spivack, G. and Shure, M.B. (1974) *Social Adjustment of Young Children*. Jersey Press: San Francisco.

Stephenson, P. and Smith, D. (1987) Anatomy of a playground bully. *Education,* 18 Sept. 1987, 236-237.

Stevenson-Hinde, J., Hinde, R.A. and Simpson, A.E. (1986) Behaviour at home and friendly or hostile behaviour in preschool. In Olweus, D., Block, J. and Radke-Yarrow, M. (eds.) *Development of Antisocial and Prosocial Behaviour: research, theories and issues.* Academic Press: New York.

Stevenson-Hinde, J. and Simpson, A.E. (1982) Temperament and relationships. In Ciba Foundation Symposium 89, *Temperamental Differences in Infants and Young Children.* Pitman Books.

Walker, J.E. and Shea, T.M. (1976) *Behaviour Modification: a practical approach for educators.* C.V. Mosby: St Louis.

Webb, L. (1969) *Children with Special Needs in the Infants' School.* Fontana Books.

Westmacott, E.V.S. and Cameron, R.J. (1981) *Behaviour Can Change.* Globe Education: Basingstoke.

Yule, W. (1970) Personal Communication.

Yule, W., Berger, M. and Wigley, V. (1984) Behaviour modification and classroom management. In Frude, N. and Gault, H. (eds.) *Disruptive Behaviour in Schools.* John Wiley.

Chapter 4
Bullying in the Junior School
Pete Stephenson and Dave Smith

Introduction

It might be said that bullying is like the proverbial elephant; difficult to describe but, by golly, you know it when you come across it. Difficult though it is to define, it is a major problem. Indeed one factor that may have contributed to the lack of research interest in Britain on bullying is that the term itself is considered suspect.

Bullying is viewed by the authors as a form of social interaction in which a more dominant individual (the bully) exhibits aggressive behaviour which is intended to and does, in fact, cause distress to a less dominant individual (the victim). The aggressive behaviour may take the form of a direct physical and/or verbal attack or may be indirect as when the bully hides a possession that belongs to the victim or spreads false information about the victim. More than one bully and more than one victim may participate in the interaction.

This definition indicates that bullying is considered to be a form of aggressive behaviour with well-defined roles which prescribe the behaviour of the victim as well as that of the bully. It is not only necessary that the bully exhibits aggressive behaviour which is intended to cause distress, it is also necessary that the victim experiences distress. In other words, it is necessary that the victim does not successfully defend himself/herself from the attack.

The definition makes explicit the unequal nature of the conflict. The bully has higher dominance status and will inevitably be the victor. The victim has lower dominance status and will inevitably be the loser. It is in this sense that bullying is an abuse of power. Dominance status and hierarchies have been investigated in a number of studies and there is evidence that reasonable stable dominance hierarchies are established among children at school from the age of about five onwards (Sluckin and Smith, 1977).

The definition also makes explicit that the aggressive behaviour exhibited by the bully is intentional. If the aggressor displayed tantrum behaviour associated with loss of self-control, the interaction should not, in our view, be defined as bullying. It is, of course, possible that the victim may display tantrum behaviour. Indeed it may well be the intention of the bully to provoke the victim to display tantrum behaviour.

Bullying as defined here is somewhat similar to the notion of harassment as described by Manning, Heron and Marshall (1978). They view harassment as a form of aggression which

> appears unprovoked, at least in the immediate situation and is directed at a person, often the same person repeatedly.

There is evidence that bullying is often longstanding, that it is often directed at the same individual repeatedly and that it often appears unprovoked in the immediate situation. These are not, however, considered to be defining characteristics. In some cases bullying is short-lived, not long-standing; in some cases it is directed against a number of different individuals, not the same individual repeatedly; and in some cases the bullying is provoked by the victim.

Bullying as defined here is also somewhat similar to the notion of hostile aggression (Fleshbach, 1964; 1970). It is likely that in many cases the sole goal of bullying is to cause distress to the victim and that it is not the means to obtain some other goal such as defending persons or property. In some cases, however, the behaviour exhibited by the bully, though intended to cause distress, may have additional goals, for example bolstering dominance status within the peer group. In what we term 'exploitative bullying', which includes extortion and blackmail, the additional goal of securing financial material, sexual or other benefit is a core component.

The Cleveland Project

Several aspects of bullying among school children have been investigated within Cleveland over a number of years. Firstly, information has been obtained on the incidence of bullying. Secondly, information has been obtained on the characteristics of bullying and on associated factors. Thirdly, teachers, children and the staff of a Psychological Service have been asked to express their views on bullying and on ways of dealing with it.

In most of the studies, the focus has been on bullying among primary school children and in particular on bullying among final year primary school children. In 1986 a study was carried out which investigated the extent and nature of bullying among secondary school aged children placed at EBD Schools (Schools for children with emotional and behavioural difficulties) and at CHE's (Community Homes with Education). This study will not be described in detail as it concerned bullying among secondary school aged children but reference will be made to it where appropriate.

The 1982 Survey

Information was collected from the teachers of final year primary school children in twenty-six schools. Use was made of measures of deprivation in the admission zones of schools to ensure that the schools selected were a representative socio-economic mix.

Two questionnaires were administered. The first questionnaire asked the teachers to rate every child in their class on a number of variables relating to, for example, behaviour, attitudes, attainments, home background and physical appearance. The teachers were asked to answer additional questions if the child was said to bully or to be bullied by other children. The additional questions enquired about the severity and form that the bullying took. Altogether information was collected from 49 teachers on 1,078 children.

The second questionnaire asked the teachers to provide information about the school and its organization, enquired about the teacher's experience of and attitude towards bullying and asked the teachers to rate the helpfulness of various courses of action in dealing with bullying problems. This questionnaire was also administered to the staff of the local Psychological Service (16 Educational Psychologists and 7 Social Workers).

In addition, a more detailed investigation was made of the six schools with the highest and the six schools with the lowest incidence of bullying.

It is stressed that information was obtained only from teachers, not from children, in the 1982 Survey.

The 1984 Single School Study

In this study bullying among the 143 children in the top two year groups in one primary school was investigated.

Information was obtained from the teachers using similar questionnaires to those used in the 1982 Survey. In this study, however, information was also collected from the children. Each child was asked:—

Does anybody in your class bully other children?   If so, who?
Does anybody in your class get bullied by other children?   If so, who?
Would you tell anybody if you were being bullied?   If so, who?
Where does bullying take place?
What should be done about bullying?

A sociometric technique was used to investigate social relationships in the classes.

It is noted that there was a high level of agreement between the nominations made by the teachers and children in this study as to which children were involved in bullying (Correlation = .8). Olewus has also reported high levels of agreement between the nominations made by children of this age and their teachers (Olweus, 1978).

Extent and Nature of Bullying

How frequent is it?

The 1982 Survey indicates that bullying is a common occurrence among final year primary school children. Twenty-three per cent of the children were said to be involved in bullying as either victims or bullies. The findings also suggest that bullying problems tend to be persistent. There were instances where the problem was said to be of recent origin but these were surprisingly few. In the majority of cases the bullying was said to have been going on for at least a year. Eighty-nine per cent of the bullies were said to have started bullying at least a year ago and 72 per cent of the victims were said to have been subjected to bullying for at least a year. It appears that bullying is not a problem that 'sorts itself out'.

An additional, though predictable, finding is that the bullying was reported to be more common among the boys than the girls. The bullies were more often boys (68 per cent), the victims were more often boys (63 per cent) and children who both bullied and were themselves bullied were more often boys (65 per cent).

The Study carried out in 1986 is of interest in the present context in that the incidence of bullying problems among children admitted to EBD schools and

CHE's was investigated. Research has suggested that there is a close relationship between bullying and other types of behavioural difficulty. The Isle of Wight study indicated that there is an association between bullying and 'conduct disordered' but not 'neurotic' behaviour, (Rutter, Tizard and Whitmore, 1970). Research carried out by West and Farrington also indicated that there is a close association between bullying and delinquency (West and Farrington, 1973). See also David Lane's chapter in this volume.

It was predicted on the basis of these studies that there would be a high incidence of bullying problems among children admitted to EBD Schools and CHE's. In fact, 65 per cent of children placed residentially in the EBD Schools and 60 per cent of children placed at the CHE's were reported to have been involved in bullying prior to admission. These figures are higher than would be expected in the population as a whole and confirm previous research findings. Of these children, approximately 45 per cent were said to bully, approximately seven per cent were said to be bullied and approximately 12 per cent were said to be both bullies and victims.

What form does bullying take?

The 1982 Survey indicates that bullying tended to be persistent. It was also reported, however, that it tended to occur in phases (75 per cent of the bullies had phases when they bullied and 77 per cent of the victims were bullied in phases). Approximately 55 per cent of both the bullies and victims were said to be involved in bullying incidents less than once a week; approximately 20 per cent of the bullies and victims were said to be involved in bullying incidents at least two or three times a week.

The majority of bullies picked on more than one child (67 per cent) and had picked on different victims at different periods of time (78 per cent). Similarly, the majority of the victims were bullied by more than one child and had been bullied by different children at different periods of time. It was reported that 41 per cent of the bullies encouraged other children to join them in bullying.

An additional finding is that the nature of the bullying tended to be different for the boys and girls. The girls more often employed, and were subjected to, verbal bullying, whereas the boys more often employed, and were subjected to, physical or a combination of both physical and verbal bullying. Fifty-six per cent of the girls who bullied employed mainly verbal methods compared to only 17 per cent of the boys. Similarly, 79 per cent of the girls who were bullied were subjected to mainly verbal bullying compared to only 40 per cent of the boys. Case studies suggest that girls frequently engage in indirect bullying, for example, the apparent practical joke or the conducting of campaigns against a particular child.

It needs to be added that the 1986 Study indicated that there was a small number of highly aggressive girls placed at both the EBD Schols and the CHE's. These girls were amongst the most aggressive children in these settings and a number of them had participated in bullying episodes of an extreme nature. Examination of the children's files suggests the possibility that teachers and other adults have more difficulty in coming to terms with extreme behaviour exhibited by girls rather than boys.

Bullying and other variables

Home and social background

Ratings made by the teachers in the 1982 Survey indicate that children involved in bullying are about three times more likely to have problems at home. Thirty per cent of the bullies, 27 per cent of the victims and 30 per cent of the bully/ victims (that is children who both bullied and were themselves bullied) were said to have problems at home. Only three per cent of the children who were not involved in bullying were reported to have problems at home.

The 1986 Study investigated the home backgrounds of the children involved in bullying. The main finding is that the home backgrounds were exceptionally problematic. Frequent references are made to the lack of firm, consistent discipline, to child-parent relationship difficulties, to family and marital difficulties and to financial and social problems. The home backgrounds of the bullies, victims and bully/victims were compared but no clear-cut differences emerged.

The 1982 Survey is of interest in that it indicates a significant relationship between bullying and social deprivation. The incidence of bullying was higher in schools located in more socially deprived areas. The schools categorised as having a high level of deprivation, had on average seven children in each class who were involved in bullying. The schools categorised as having a medium level of deprivation, had on average five children in each class who were involved, whereas the schools categorised as having a low level of deprivation had, on average, two children in each class who were involved.

School factors

The 1982 Survey suggests that bullying occurs much more frequently in some schools than others. In three schools there was said to be no bullying at all among the final year children. In about a quarter of the schools, 30 per cent or more of the year group were reported to be involved and in one school over 50 per cent of the year group. Bullying tended to be more prevalent in the larger schools and in schools which had larger classes though the differences were not statistically significant.

Additional study was made of the six schools with the highest and the six schools with the lowest incidence of bullying. In all but one of the low bullying schools the teachers expressed articulate, considered and also purposeful views on bullying which emphasized the need for prevention whereas this was less apparent in the high bullying schools. The responses suggest that there was an agreed policy on bullying in the low bullying schools. The following are representative statements made by teachers in low and high bullying schools.

Low Bullying Schools

We do not accept bullying. We observe very carefully, particularly children admitted from other schools and stress that we are all friends and live happily together. A stern warning is given to any child who shows any sign of aggressive behaviour. The child is reminded what behaviour is expected and is helped to achieve this.

High Bullying Schools

'It is not possible to generalize — we use a variety of approaches. We attempt to reason with the bully'.

'Take away privileges. Show affection to both the bully and the victim. A good telling-off. A do-as-you-would-be-done-unto approach'.

It is notable that two of the three schools which reported a complete absence of bullying were unusually small schools which both employed cross-age grouping of pupils. One of the teachers expressed the view that cross-age grouping encourages a more caring and less competitive ethos among children and that this discourages the emergence of bullying.

Though the majority of the low bullying schools were situated in less disadvantaged areas and tended to have smaller classes and to be smaller schools, there were exceptions. Indeed the school with the highest score on the measure of deprivation also had the largest class size of all the schools but was a low bullying school.

Children in the 1984 Study were asked to state where and when bullying takes place. The majority of responses followed a clear pattern. Most bullying was said to take place on the playground and school field and it is of interest that several responses specified particular areas of the playground and field. Bullying was also said to take place in dinner queues and in the classroom, while travelling to and from school and in a variety of other locations outside the school. The responses suggest that most bullying takes place during school hours at times when children are less closely supervised and when the children are in relatively large groups playing rough-and-tumble or competitive games.

Physical Characteristics of the Children

Educational folklore suggests that children are bullied because they are different or deviant in some way. It is assumed that any child who differs from the norm is a potential target for bullying. Research carried out by Olweus indicates that this is not so (Olweus 1978). He found that children who are not bullied are as likely to be deviant in some way as children who are bullied. He concludes that children are not singled out for bullying because they are deviant but that bullies might well latch on to some oddity in a potential victim as a pretext for bullying.

The findings in the 1982 Survey are not clear-cut on this issue. On the one hand there are no differences between any of the groups as regards the prevalence of physical defects. On the other hand, victims of bullying were more often rated as being 'thin' and as 'appearing different from the rest of the class for example in dress and speech' (18 per cent of the victims, 15 per cent of the bully/victims, three per cent of the bullies and three per cent of the children not involved in bullying were rated as appearing different from the rest of the class). The victims were rated as having poor personal hygiene but so also were the bullies. Further research is necessary to determine in what ways victims, and indeed bullies and bully/victims, differ in their physical characteristics from children who are not bullied.

The Participants

The interactions we have defined as bullying are not isolated, infrequent occurrences but exist in a large number of schools and involve a large number of children. What then are the defining characteristics, if any, of the bully and the victim? What makes them different from the majority of children in school who are not involved in bullying? Indeed, are there any differences and if so can these give clues as to the reasons for the phenomenon and perhaps indicate ways of overcoming the problems of the children and the problems they pose within the school organization?

Bullying is traditionally viewed as a conflict between the stereotypic, cowardly bully and the weak, 'somehow different' victim. Data collected from the 1982 Survey suggests that this view is an over-simplification. In fact, distinct sub-groups of both bullies and victims were identified. Within the group identified as bullies, there is a small sub-group we have termed 'anxious-bullies' and within the group identified as victims, there is a small sub-group we have termed 'provocative victims'. There is also a group of children who were identified as being both bullies and victims and we have labelled these children 'bully/victims'.

It is stressed that all these groups of children have characteristics in common. Children in all the groups have poorer school attainments, poorer concentration and below average personal hygiene compared with the children not involved in bullying. They are also rated as being three times more likely to have problems at home. In effect all the children involved in bullying have in common is that they are disadvantaged.

Bullies

About one in ten of the sample were described as currently bullying other children. A traditional explanation of the behaviour of bullies is that they are insecure, unpopular children and that their bullying is an attempt to compensate for this. The Survey findings do indicate that they are the physically strongest of all the groups, that they are active and assertive, and that they are easily provoked and enjoy situations which have an aggressive content. There is no suggestion, however, that they are insecure or unpopular. The ratings indicate that they are of average popularity with other children and that they are the most confident of all the groups of children. A positive attitude to violence rather than insecurity or unpopularity most likely underlies the behaviour.

Anxious Bullies

Within the group of bullies, a small number (18 per cent) were found to have very different characteristics. This group is composed almost entirely of boys. They are said to be less popular with other children than the main group of bullies and are said to be the least confident of all the groups. They are reported to have fewer likeable qualities and more frequently have problems at home. In addition they are rated as having the poorest school attainments and poorest concentration of all the groups. We have labelled these children 'anxious bullies'.

In a number of respects the children in this group conform to the traditional view of the bully. They are rated as being insecure and unpopular, with marked educational difficulties and their bullying may well be an attempt to compensate for feelings of inadequacy. In this context bullies are sometimes portrayed in fictional stories as being 'ignorant oafs' who give vent to repeated experiences of failure at school by bullying. The 1986 Study also showed that a considerable number of the bullies at EBD Schools were anxious bullies. It is stressed, however, that only a minority of bullies fall within this category. It is only this minority who conform to the traditional view of the bully.

Victims

Seven per cent of the total sample were found to be currently the subjects of bullying. The majority of these children are rated as being passive individuals, as lacking self-confidence and as being unpopular with other children. They are also rated as being physically weaker than the other children.

It is further reported that a considerable number of the victims did not tell their teachers they were being bullied. Indeed the ratings indicate that 22 per cent of the victims never told their teacher and 59 per cent only occasionally told their teacher they were being bullied.

Provocative Victims

There is no suggestion that the group of victims as a whole provoke antagonism amongst their peers and actively enjoy aggressive situations and yet for a small group (17 per cent), this does appear to be the case. We have labelled these children 'provocative victims'. They are rated as being more active, assertive and confident than other victims, as being physically stronger and as being easily provoked. The findings also indicate that they more often complain to their teachers that they are being bullied even though it appears that they actively provoke the bullying. Provocative victims often create considerable management difficulties for teachers. The teacher is frequently placed in the situation of having to decide whether the provocative victim did, in fact, provoke the bullying and this sometimes necessitates the expenditure of considerable time and effort.

Bully/Victims

It is often assumed that children are either bullies or are victims. The Survey findings indicate that there is, in fact, a small group of children who both bully and who are themselves bullied. Six per cent of the total sample fall into this group and we have called them 'bully/victims'. These children are rated as being the least popular with other children of all the groups identified. They are physically stronger and more assertive than the victims. Like the anxious bullies and provocative bullies they are very easily provoked and frequently provoke others.

A Variety of Viewpoints

Teachers, children and the staff of the Psychological Service were asked to express their views on bullying and on ways of dealing with it.

Attitudes to Bullying

The 1982 Survey indicates that bullying is a common occurrence among children. Approximately a quarter of the children were found to be involved in the phenomenon. This suggests, perhaps, that bullying is an inevitable and unexceptional apect of life at school. There is indeed some suggestion that many of the teachers who participated in the 1982 Survey consider bullying to be a fairly unexceptional behaviour. Ninety-one per cent of the teachers who said that they had a bullying problem in their class described it as being of a 'minor' nature. The results indicate, however, that the bullying frequently involved physical aggression, had usually been going on for about a year or longer and in about a quarter of cases occurred several times a week. A considerable deal of stress and suffering is suggested by these findings.

Twenty-five per cent of the teachers in the Survey stated that it is sometimes helpful to ignore bullying problems, as doing something about it is likely to make it more of a problem. Yet the majority of the children interviewed in the 1984 Study looked to adults to do something about it. Over half the children looked to their teachers to take action and about a quarter looked to their parents to take action. It is notable that in three classes nearly all the children said they would tell somebody if they were being bullied. In the remaining class, seven children said they would tell nobody. One possibility is that the statements made by the children in this class reflected differing attitudes to bullying on the part of the teachers.

Attitudes to Intervention Approaches

The findings indicate that teachers and the staff of the Psychological Service agree as to the effectiveness of some intervention approaches but disagree as to the effectiveness of other approaches. There is a high level of agreement that involving parents is helpful. There is also a fair measure of agreement that encouraging peer group disapproval of bullying is useful. There is disagreement, however, as to the value of talking to children and as to the value of verbal reprimands. The techniques most favoured by the teachers were use of verbal reprimands to deter the bully and attempting to change the bully's behaviour by reasoning with him/her. The staff of the Psychological Service preferred a more behavioural approach. The favoured approaches were encouraging the victim to become more assertive, increasing the prestige of the victim within the class and rewarding non-aggressive behaviour. It is notable that two of the techniques favoured by the Psychological Service focused on changing the behaviour of the victim rather than that of the bully. Use of physical punishment to deter the bully was considered to be sometimes helpful by about half the teachers and about a third of the staff of the Psychological Service.

The majority of children interviewed in the Single School Study advocated the use of punishment as an intervention technique. The victim or another child should tell their teacher what is happening and the teacher should then punish the bully. The full gamut of punishments is suggested, from being told-off to being sent to a 'prison school'. Other children suggested that there should be more supervision by teachers at times of the day when bullying was most likely to take place. Several children indicated that they would fight the bully or get friends or even another bully to help them.

What Can Be Done?

Summary of Findings

The extent and nature of bullying among final year primary school children have been investigated and attitudes to bullying and ways of dealing with it explored.

The findings suggest that bullying is a common occurrence among children of this age and that it persists over a considerable period of time. Approximately a quarter of the children were involved in bullying and it had been going on for at least a year in about three-quarters of the cases.

The findings also suggest that it is a complex problem. Firstly, distinct subgroups of both bullies and victims were identified and some children were reported both to bully other children and to be themselves bullied. Secondly, variables at the class, school, family and community, as well as at the individual level, were found to influence bullying. Failure to take this complexity into account may explain the ineffectiveness of traditional approaches to dealing with bullying.

The Need for Assessment

What then is to be done in response to bullying? Firstly, it is necessary for the seriousness of bullying as a problem to be acknowledged. Children have the right to expect that they will not be subjected to bullying and neither they nor their parents should have to feel anxious about the possibility of its occurrence. If this is not accepted within a school, action needs to be taken to increase staff awareness of the necessity of effectively tackling the problem. It is necessary that teachers are vigilant for the signs of distress that may indicate that a child is being bullied.

Secondly, an assessment should be carried out to indicate whether or not bullying is a problem. Indeed it is suggested that this should be done on a regular basis as a preventative measure. If bullying is, in fact, shown to be a problem, a more detailed assessment should be made of factors that may be influencing the bullying at each of the levels. Use might be made of assessment techniques similar to those used in the 1982 Survey and 1984 Single School Study, backed up by careful observation by the teacher. The effectiveness of intervention will be largely determined by the thoroughness of the assessment made at each level.

At the individual level an assessment should be made of the characteristics of the children involved. Detailed investigation should also be made into occurrences of bullying. The '5-W' questions might well form the basis of such an enquiry, (What? Who? Where? When? Why?). The answers given to these questions will have bearing on the responses made to bullying not only at the individual but at the other levels as well.

At the class level, an assessment should be made of the nature of the relationships between the children and of the nature of the relationship between the teacher and the children. In this context the methods of control used by the teacher and the nature of the classroom rules and their acceptance by the children is of particular relevance. Aspects of classroom organization such as seating and supervision arrangements should be considered. All the children involved in bullying tend to have below average school attainments and concentration. This suggests that attention should also be given to assessing factors related to the curriculum.

At the school level, the nature of the school ethos and organization is of primary concern. Factors such as the school disciplinary policy and how it is determined are relevant in this context. Assessment should also be made of the adequacy of supervision arrangements, particularly at times and in places where bullying may occur.

At the community level, the nature of the relationship between the school and parents, and between the school and the local community, should be investigated. The use made by the school of advisory services within the Education and other Departments should also be noted.

Intervention Approaches

If assessment carried out at the individual level indicates that an anxious bully or a provocative victim is involved, a main focus of the intervention should be to help these children. It is worth noting here that if one or both of these types of children are involved in a bullying interaction, the situation is likely to be especially problematic. With provocative victims, the initial need is to demonstrate to them that it is their own behaviour that is provoking the aggression. Once this is achieved, steps can be taken to discourage the provocative and to encourage alternative behaviour. With anxious bullies, action may well need to be taken to improve their self-confidence, self-esteem, social skills and also educational attainments. It is especially important to engage the co-operation of the parents of these children.

With other victims, possible goals might be to encourage the development of assertiveness, self-confidence and of social and friendship skills. The aggressive behaviour exhibited by bullies and bully/victims is not easily modified. It is suggested that aggressive behaviour should be actively discouraged by, for example, loss of privileges. At the same time non-aggressive behaviour should be actively encouraged by, for example, encouraging the bully to take on a tutoring or caring role with younger children.

At the classroom level, consideration might be given to incorporating discussion of bullying into the curriculum. Use might be made of appropriate study materials to stimulate discussion. Strategies that might be adopted if confronted with aggressive behaviour could then be role-played. The intention is that bullying is brought into the open and made a subject for discussion rather than being viewed as a phenomenon to be tolerated. (See Graham Herbert's contribution in Chapter 6).

At the level of the school, consideration might need to be given to changing the school ethos. It is suggested that the ethos should be one in which non-violence, respect for others and mutual support is encouraged. It is further suggested that there needs to be a whole-school disciplinary policy accepted by both staff and children which makes explicit reference to bullying. Finally, there needs to be adequate monitoring and supervision arrangements, for example, a system of spot-checks could be introduced. The role of supervisory as well as teaching staff need to be incorporated in these arrangements.

At the community level, communication between the school and parents and between the school and the local community may need to be improved. If it is indeed the case, as suggested by the 1982 Survey, that there is a relationship between bullying in schools and level of deprivation, the establishment of close links between the school and the various welfare agencies is likely to be of benefit.

Generally speaking, it is suggested that approaches to dealing with bullying should emphasize both control and prevention. The aim of control being to reduce and, hopefully, eliminate the occurrence of bullying; the aim of prevention being to bring about conditions in which bullying is unlikely to occur in the future. If a response to bullying is to have preventative as well as control value, action may need to be taken not only at the individual but also at the other levels of intervention. The optimally constructive response to bullying is likely to be multi-level.

Notes

1. The views expressed in this chapter are those of the authors and not necessarily those of their employing authorities.
2. The authors acknowledge the help provided by teachers, staff of the Cleveland Psychological Service, other colleagues and also children. In particular we acknowledge the help given by Gill Rollings of Cleveland County Research and Intelligence and by Colin Newton, Educational Psychologist.

References

Feshbach, S., (1964) 'The function of aggression and the regulation of the aggressive drive', *Psychological Review* 71, 257-272.

Feshbach, S., (1970) Aggression. In P.H. Mussen (ed.), Revision of Carmichael's *Manual of Child Psychology,* vol, 2, 159-259. Wiley, New York.

Manning, M., Heron, J., and Marshall, T., (1978) Styles of hostility and social interactions at nursery, at school and at home. In L.A. Hersov and M. Berger (eds.), *Aggression and anti-social behaviour in childhood and adolescence.* Pergamon.

Olweus, D., (1978) *Aggression in the schools: bullies and whipping boys.* Hemisphere, Washington D.C.

Rutter, M., Tizard, J., and Whitmore, K. (eds.), (1970) *Education, health and behaviour,* Longman.

Sluckin, A.M., and Smith, P.H., (1977) 'Two approaches to the concept of dominance in pre-school children', *Child Development,* 48, 917-923.

Stephenson, P., and Smith, D., (1987) 'Anatomy of the playground bully', *Education* 18 Aug. 1987, 236-237.

West, D.J., and Farrington, D.P., (1973) *Who becomes delinquent?* Heinemann.

Chapter 5
Aggressive behaviour in boys: to what extent is it institutionalised?

Sue Askew

Bullying and aggressive behaviour are widespread problems in both primary and secondary schools. Other chapters in this book have indicated the extent of the problem and have suggested some underlying explanations as to the causes. Clearly any attempt to understand bullying and aggressive behaviour must involve explanations which focus on the individual child — whether bully or victim — and attempts to locate this behaviour at the individual, psychological level are invaluable in dealing with it. However, it is argued that this explanation is one element in a very complex situation. This chapter will attempt to focus on another element; the institution. In doing so it will highlight ways in which the school as an institution may unintentionally either reinforce or discourage this behaviour. It will also outline some strategies which have been developed in some schools to deal with bullying.

The research (Askew & Ross, 1988) on which this chapter is based was conducted with boys as the primary focus and much of it was carried out in single-sex boys' schools. It did not begin with a focus on bullying or aggression but on boys' experiences of single-sex schools and women teachers' experiences of teaching in them. The author has worked in approximately thirty boys' schools and twenty mixed schools in one Education Authority and ran workshops to which over two hundred teachers from all kinds of schools came. These teachers were largely concerned with one thing: the 'problem' of the boys. This problem was usually presented as worry about the amount of aggression between boys and the demands made on teachers by boys. It is recognised that girls also bully and may be aggressive both towards one another and towards their teachers. However, research has shown that bullying among boys is significantly higher than among girls (Olweus, 1978). This chapter focuses on boys and boys' schools because it is argued that an examination of the issues surrounding the education of boys will help to illuminate prevailing structures in all educational systems. Boys' socialisation and education has direct implications for girls' education. Thus, it is argued, *all* schools perpetuate the values and ideologies of the dominant groups in society. In this society, therefore, the values of schools as institutions to a greater or lesser extent will reflect and reinforce stereotypes of masculinity. Because of the 'all-male' atmosphere of a boys' school, these stereotypes and values are more apparent in them, but will nevertheless exist in all educational institutions. These 'stereotypes' are consistent with and, indeed, underlie bullying and aggressive behaviour.

Observing boys in school

There is a good deal of evidence to show that boys demand and are given a greater proportion of teacher attention in both primary and secondary mixed schools (Carricoates, 1978; Stanworth, 1981; Walkerdine, 1981). Tingle (1985) writes about his experience as an English teacher when boys were amalgamated into a girls' secondary school:

> The boys plunge into things, interrupt discussion, can't keep still, can't wait. Ten boys in a class of 29 and they demand 50% or more of my time. Yet the work they produce is often shallow, non-reflective and is always messy . . . The boys in protective groups, generally resist giving anything of themselves. They hide their feelings, they joke, they are loud, they are very physical.

The 'physicality' of boys is something about which teachers in this research referred to constantly. For example,

> The thing which struck me most forcibly when I came here (to a boys' school from a co-education school) was the way in which the boys could not leave one another alone. Especially the younger boys of 11, 12 and 13. They seem to punch one another as a general way of communicating. They will sit getting on with their work when suddenly someone will poke, tug at or hit his neighbour for absolutely no apparent reason.

Worries were also commonly expressed about physicality in the playground. These comments were largely made by teachers of primary age children and this may reflect teachers' greater knowledge and awareness of individual children and their behaviours in a primary school, rather than the lack of such behaviour in secondary school:

> We are constantly trying to address the problem of playground behaviour. We are most concerned about the way the boys' games take up all the playground space while the girls are relegated to the edges. Children themselves are always telling us about fights in the playground and being picked on. We've been doing our own observation as part of a project on the playground and it does seem from this observation that it's mainly boys who run around, hit one another and fight.

The author's own data compiled from observations and discussions with boys in a boys' school over a four year period concentrated on the ways boys interrelate. For example, observing collaborative learning activities, the ways boys relate to each other, to men and women teachers, to different subjects and different teaching styles. The boys observed (who were from a variety of cultural, ethnic and class backgrounds) seemed to relate to one another in very rigid, stylised and competitive ways. Many of the boys demonstrated a general lack of trust and support towards one another. They were, for the most part guarded towards each other and their talk seemed to revolve around very impersonal subject matter. There was considerable non-verbal, aggressive or physical communication among boys. 'Body language' such as stance or tone of voice played a large part in interaction. Physicality was not only used as a means of intimidation between the boys, but also as a way of making social contact. Conflicts over such things as whose turn it was to use some materials, or how to go about a joint task, would often be expressed and decided in physical terms (for example, by a push or a shove). A good deal of talk among boys in the classroom was to do with issuing challenges or 'put-downs' to each other. It was also apparent that many boys found it extremely difficult to listen to one another. They would respond to one another's answers in class with contradiction, derision or direct challenge. More often, they would simply not bother to listen, especially if they themselves had something to say.

Some behaviour described so far is implicitly aggressive. However, there is also a great deal of explicitly aggressive behaviour among boys at school. Observation in a variety of schools showed that boys from a variety of social class and ethnic groups were involved in bullying or aggressive behaviour. In addition there was much racist bullying specifically affecting children from ethnic minority groups.

Apart from physical aggression, a great deal of verbal abuse was heard. This was so common as to become part of 'normal' speech. Much of the verbal abuse was homophobic, reflecting the oppression and fear of gay people in the school and society generally; other abuse was related to physical stature or general appearance, including dress.

While some teachers viewed this behaviour as problematic, it was also considerable cause for anxiety among the boys themselves:

I keep a low profile, keep myself to myself really. There's always some kind of trouble going on, but I keep out of it if I can.

In a class discussion with a group of fifth years about their experiences at the school many of them were very angry about aggressive behaviour amongst themselves. Below are some comments recorded during the discussion:

It's meant some really clever kids have just given up. Look at Shafic, Wayne and Obu. They don't bother any more.

Our class have been really bad since the first year and no-one's done anything about it. It's mainly one or two boys, but it affects everyone. You think, 'Oh well, better him than me' and you just join in.

You always feel you have to be careful. Most people have got picked on at some time or other. You always feel you might be next.

These boys were angry that the situation had been allowed to continue for five years and that it had negatively affected their school work. They were clearly saying that they wanted to work and wanted the bullying behaviour to stop, but had not felt supported by the school.

The definition of bullying in itself is problematic and may involve the prescription that to be defined as such it must involve long term abuse occurring on a regular basis. However, it is argued here that bullying should be regarded as a *continuum* of behaviour which involves the attempt to gain power and dominance over another. While long-term bullying will certainly have serious and painful consequences, particularly for the victim, *all* behaviour which involves power relationships and struggles between pupils will have negative consequences both for the pupils' feeling of safety and for learning. As such, it is argued, the kinds of behaviour described cannot be considered as 'boys just learning to be boys'. Additionally this behaviour does not only affect a 'small' percentage of children either bullied or bullies — on the contrary it affects everyone in the classroom

Stereotypes of Masculinity

Not all boys are demanding and aggressive. Indeed the number of boys in any one class who are may be small. However, it is important that it is *boys* who are thus perceived by teachers rather than girls. This section focuses on how masculinity is constructed in our society. There is a dominant image of men portrayed in the media as strong, independent, brave, rational, tough, sexually active, intelligent, rational and aggressive. These stereotypical traits are not neutral. On the contrary they are generally thought to be 'good' and worthwhile. A large sample in America (Archer and Lloyd, 1982) in the 1970's listed the following as both masculine *and* desirable: very dominant, always hiding emotions, very objective, very independent, very competitive, never crying, very ambitious and very aggressive. This study also showed that, on the whole, behaviour which was seen as typically 'male' was also valued much more highly than that seen as typically 'female'. Whether or not these ideas about men are true, they are the images which young boys are learning to aspire to. It is sometimes argued that such characteristics as aggression in males is 'natural'. It is clear that, whether or not it is natural, it is not a characteristic which a 'civilised' society would want to promote. Because it is argued that something is natural it does not follow that it is either immutable or desirable. There is, however, a strong argument to be made for 'masculine' behaviour being learned. For example, research at the University of Sussex (Smith and Lloyd, 1978) has indicated that parents interpret the same behaviour differently depending on whether they *think* the baby is a boy or a girl and consequently reward the behaviour differently. Media influences are strong and recent Home Office research shows that children do indeed copy behaviour they see on television.

The majority of reports dealing with aggression in young children have been concerned with nursery schools. They have also largely focused on middle-class boys (Archer and Lloyd, 1982). In more than twenty investigations published before 1966, boys were observed to be more aggressive than girls. More recent studies in Britain have shown similar results. Aggression has also been studied in children by setting up laboratory situations. For example, in one such study (Nicholson, 1984) a group of eight-year-olds were told that a child in the next room was working on arithmetic problems and asked to help by pressing a button every time a wrong answer was given. The button would mean that the child would be hit with a punching-machine. They were told this would help the child learn. The children were told from time to time that the 'victim' had made a mistake and pressed buttons which were supposed to deliver blows — number one button giving a soft punch, number two a medium punch and number three a hard punch. Boys chose to inflict significantly more pain on their non-existent victims than girls. Nicholson (1984) comments:

> What really seems to hold women back is that they feel much more strongly than men that they ought not to behave aggressively, and become much more anxious after behaving aggressively unless they have some justification for their action . . . the circumstances in which women show aggression are very different; either there is a matter of principle involved, or else they see someone else treated unfairly.

It is argued that toughness and aggression are approved of in boys: boys are encouraged to be tough and stick up for themselves. Boys may be rewarded with parental approval for being rough: 'I like the way he's rough. He's a proper lad' remarked one mother about her four year old son to Newson and Newson (1984). This is not usually meant as an open encouragement for boys to be violent, more of a message that violence is all right if not taken too far. It is an appropriate way of looking after yourself and can in many circumstances improve social status with other boys. Perhaps the most important message for boys is that they must at all cost avoid being thought afraid to fight. The next section looks at the ways in which schools too may reinforce these messages about masculinity.

The school ethos and organisation

It has been shown that boys' behaviour may be problematic. It is now argued that in exploring the roots of the problem it is necessary to focus not only on the behaviour itself, but on the structure and organisation of the school system.

Some research has pointed to the relationship between aggressive behaviour and the school organisation, policies on discipline and teaching methods:

> The many elements that comprise the ethos of the school can perpetuate and, indeed, create the aggression a school seeks to control . . . There is a clear need for research in boys' schools into such things as the forms and manner of discipline; teaching styles; teacher expectations of pupil behaviour and the organisational structure of the school (Davidson, 1985).

In the author's research it was found that, whether or not discipline was characterised by authoritarian power and control through strength, boys interviewed revealed that they *think* violence will be used against them:

> He says he'll string us up if we don't get on with our work.

> We behave in his class because if not he'll hit us.

Such threats may be made with no intention of enforcing them, but nevertheless they reinforce the idea that discipline is attained by force. Some men teachers commented on the way in which they thought aggression among the boys reflected the authoritarian structures in the school:

> The whole way of relating to boys in the school stems from a blaming, punitive approach. There's a deficiency model which is very aggressive. A contradic-

tion occurs when a teacher threatens a boy with physical punishment for bullying another boy.

It's a case of how a particular classroom climate comes about. Whether you are there to educate or control. The sorts of methods by which control is achieved in our school have too often relied on an aggressive and a controlling style. I think you can see a shift in our school to sharing the power with the class so that they engage much more in their own learning. A negotiated position with real meaning means that you carry it through and don't resort to the power relationship afterwards.

I think one of the most important things is for people to become aware of how they deal with an issue like bullying. In our school it's an aggressive style if you like and a dominant style of dealing with someone who's gone against the rules. The message is 'This is how you get what you want' and I think the boys go 'Ah ha, so this is the way'.

Apart from the maintenance of discipline and authority in boys' schools by actual and threatened physical punishment, there are other ways in which boys are kept 'in check', that also rely on power and strength: for example, loud shouting to 'shut up' or sarcasm. There is often peer group pressure on boys to be aggressive, yet discipline appears to be commonly dealt with in an individual 'crisis orientated' way. Involving the class in the discussion of solutions was rare in classes observed. The Head of Year or House was often called into the class to reprimand the boys. In these cases the classroom teacher clearly needed the support of the senior teachers, but the message seemed to be that responsibility for behaviour lay with the teacher powerful enough to reinforce it. This attitude denies the possibility of self-discipline or of pupil co-operation for their own self-interest or out of consideration for others. It also has implications for power dynamics between people generally.

It has been suggested by other researchers O'Hagan & Edmunds (1982) that aggressive disciplinary methods, while appearing initially to be effective in controlling misbehaviour, could well have negative consequences in other ways: for example, by increasing the likelihood of truancy.

Competitiveness appeared to be another major element of the boys' schools. Several teachers commented on the competitive ethos of the boys' school in which they worked compared with mixed schools in which they had worked:

Competitiveness is a thread running through the ways boys relate to one another. It's very hard to establish collaborative work in this school and that's partly to do with the fact that collaborative work has never really been very highly valued or encouraged.

Competitiveness is also aligned to the hierarchical structure by this teacher:

There seems to be a really deep kind of hierarchical structure. It seems that, in order to get to the top, you have to fight it out with your colleagues. The more you go up the further you seem to be removed from colleagues down there somewhere. There's a kind of psychological distance and because of this the power seems to be in terms of telling people what to do — it doesn't allow for any support to go on.

Other teachers also talked about the effects of rigidly hierarchical structures:

If there is a consultative structure then it's possible to set up situations where people are able to relate on a more equal footing and make better use of expertise. It makes you feel that you can control things more. But here if you're experiencing difficulty or feeling dissatisfied with anything that's going on you can't say so publicly. Any signs of vulnerability don't fit with that hierarchical model. The consultative model is a support model.

It has been argued that 'strength' plays an important part in the control of boys in boys' schools. It is not surprising, therefore, that many teachers talked about attitudes within their schools being uncritical of some forms of aggressive behaviour. Frequent comments were mentioned such as 'He's a Cissy', 'Boys will be boys', 'He's got to learn to take it like a man'. It follows from this that one element of bullying may be to do with the way that physical power and strength are part of stereotyped male attributes. Bullying is a major way in which boys are able to demonstrate their manliness. Even though a boy might be physically weaker than another, to be able to 'take it like a man' is usually considered to be a good second-best masculine quality. In this sense bullying can be seen as a manifestation of pressures put on boys to conform to male stereotypes. It is acknowledged that bullying also takes place among girls, but it is likely that it would take a different form since physical bullying would conflict with, rather than reinforce stereotyped notions of 'femininity'. Boys may have been socialised into accepting a very aggressive image of themselves and this may be reinforced by the norms, rules and roles of the institution. Another aspect of bullying may be the acting out of the power structures within the institution. As such, it can be seen as an acting out of power dynamics at the pupil level of the institution.

It has been argued that the values promoted by an institution will very much reflect the values of the dominant group in society. All schools are founded on similar values, but it is argued that boys' schools are more *explicitly* built on 'male' values. For example, in boys' schools it has been suggested that competitiveness is more overt. In this society a high value is placed on competitiveness and it has become one of the stereotypical traits associated with masculinity. In mixed or girls' schools the competitiveness at the basis of all education has been blurred, perhaps due to the presence of girls and a large number of female staff. This is not to say that women and girls are not competitive but that the manifestations of competition will be less extreme and therefore less visible.

Working towards collaboration

If it is accepted that one element of bullying is to do with an acting out of the power structures both of school and other institutions in society, then clearly we need to tackle bullying on several levels. There are pupils in school who can be identified as either persistent bullies or victims, usually because of family problems or personality difficulties. These children need to be referred for individual help. However, it has been demonstrated that bullying affects more children than those directly bullied or bullying. If the bullying is occurring *within* the class then if affects all the pupils in the class. If it is happening between years, then it can affect the whole year group. This means that as well as tackling bullying at the level of the individual we also need to tackle it at the level of the group and the institution. Included in this section are two short case studies as illustration of one way in which bullying was approached at both these levels in one boys' school in which the author worked.

Working in the Form Group

Four years ago I became the form tutor of a first year group of boys in an inner city boys' comprehensive school. I had already worked in the school for a year and been struck by the amount of bullying and general aggression between the boys. This seemed to affect the whole class and the work which boys were able to do in it. Because I had taught eight first year classes that year, I could see clearly that the boys' behaviour changed drastically about two weeks after they entered the school. In the first two weeks they were cheerful, friendly and open. In the third week they became guarded, surly and overly concerned with one another in an aggressive way. It seemed at the time that they were involved in sorting out a kind of hierarchy in the groups based on physical strength and competition.

When I took on my form I was determined that they should co-operate with one another — both so that the form group should have a pleasant atmosphere and, very importantly, so that pupils should be able to get on with work without feeling under threat.

Fortunately, I taught my form humanities seven periods a week as well as seeing them twice a day for registration. I decided we should get to know as much about one another as possible in the belief that the more we empathise with others, the less likely we are to hurt them. In tutor periods and in humanities, therefore, we talked about and wrote about ourselves. I introduced this by always talking about myself and writing stories about my childhood — it seems unfair to expect young people to disclose information about themselves if we as adults are not prepared to do the same. This also, of course, has an additional affect of, to some extent, breaking down the power dynamics between teacher and pupils.

We published our writing in a form booklet of which everyone had a copy and which we read aloud to one another. I also decided to make it very explicit that in our form we could co-operate and help one another. I made it clear why this was important — I explained that in my view we all learn best if we help one another; that by explaining things to someone else we understand them better ourselves. I also insisted that in the class pupils were intellectually equal although some may have had different experiences and more practice at certain things than others. I was trying to lay the ground for a development of mutual respect, if not liking (I emphasised that we could not be expected to like every member of the form group but we could certainly respect their persons and leave them alone). It was made clear to the pupils that if fighting or bullying were going on then it was *all* our problem, because it affected us all and that we had to find solutions to it. It was also understood that each time an incident occurred we could discuss it in the class and postpone the planned lesson.

Pupils in the form were thus able to bring up incidents as they occurred. I tried to facilitate an open atmosphere in which problems could be discussed and to make pupils take some responsibility for their own behaviour.

This class is now in the fifth year, about to take their GCSE exams. They have consistently been thought by other subject teachers to be a 'good' class to teach. Other pupils in different classes also comment on the relationships in the class. Many of them are expected to do very well in their examinations.

It may well be that this was a 'better' than average class, but it seems likely also that they have learned to operate in a different way because of the form tutoring they received.

Working With Teachers

Recently I had the opportunity of working with teachers on issues concerned with bullying. I was involved in facilitating workshops in one local education authority which were originally planned together with Eileen Carnell (Co-ordinator for Health Education in the ILEA). In my role as Advisory Teacher I meet a considerable number of teachers in both primary and secondary schools who express concern about the ways children relate to one another. Accordingly, a short course was run to enable teachers to develop strategies for dealing with bullying.

The course of three workshops was initially open to teachers from both single sex and co-educational secondary schools and had the following aims:—

(i)   To reach a consensus about what kinds of behaviour constitute 'bullying' and explore ways of monitoring the level of bullying in school.

(ii) To share experiences of dealing with bullying and build up a collection of useful strategies.

(iii) To identify aspects of both classroom practice and whole school policy which have an impact, positive or negative, on children's relationships.

(iv) To plan ways of initiating the develpment of school policies on bullying.

Teachers were encouraged to attend the course with colleagues from their own school wherever possible so that there would be mutual encouragement and support to initiate change. Twenty-three teachers from seven schools attended (four co-educational schools, two boys' and one girls' school).

The teachers began by working together to 'brainstorm' an ending to the following statements:

Bullying is . . .
People who bully . . .
People who get bullied . . .

The statements were shared and discussed.

Next, small groups of teachers worked on a definition of bullying. Again these were discussed in the whole group. Most teachers agreed that specific incidents keep occurring that involved the same children over a considerable time and that these might most readily be accepted as 'serious bullying'. However, it was also felt that bullying should be considered as a continuum of behaviour, ranging from 'one-off' incidents of verbal and physical assault to long-term abuse — all of it unacceptable. Several teachers stressed this point, arguing that a focus on only the most severe cases tends to minimise, if not 'normalise' the high level of general aggressive behaviour.

In the second workshop, teachers worked with colleagues from their own school to consider areas of the school where bullying takes place and the type of bullying that goes on. This lead to discussion about how to monitor and record incidents of bullying. It was thought that some methods of monitoring would work in some schools but not others and several participants agreed to try out different approaches. In one school with a well organised and developed School Council it was decided to invite members of the School Council to put bullying on the agenda for their next meeting and discuss with form representatives how they could be involved in the monitoring and what form it should take. Three teachers from another school decided to try to use a questionnaire to find out how much bullying is actually going on.

Next we looked at what action should be taken. We first shared our experiences of dealing with bullying and talked about how effective we had found our strategies to be. We focused this discussion by using prepared statements (see Appendix 1) on cards. Each participant was asked to arrange the statements according to their importance in dealing with bullying. Rather than ordering them from one to nine, they were to be arranged in a 'diamond nine' pattern (as set out in the Appendix). Participants were invited to alter the wording of the statements and add their own strategies. Individuals then compared their priorities and worked towards a consensus.

In the final session we made plans for initiating the development of a school policy. We also 'brainstormed' those areas which we agreed would need to be considered when formulating such a policy and came up with the following list:— playground, supervision, monitoring, hierarchies, discipline, pupil responsibilities, curriculum, teachers as models, suspension, others.

Some groups of teachers decided to write a short statement about the problems of bullying in their school and ask for in-service training time to present and discuss it. Other teachers wrote an account of the workshops and the issues that had arisen, so as to raise these issues in their own schools. Other teachers wanted to adapt the course workshops for colleagues in their schools.

At the end of the course, participants were asked to evaluate its usefulness. Most people had clearly found the course supportive and it had raised interesting issues for them. Equally clearly, support needs to be on-going and institutionalised. Teachers made comments such as:—

The course made me feel less isolated. I thought I was the only teacher struggling so inadequately with problems of bullying. It was very useful to share strategies with other teachers.

I feel renewed enthusiasm to go back into school and try and generate some whole school policies on bullying. It's good to have my feeling that bullying *is* a central issue in the learning process confirmed by others.

I've found the workshops very valuable, but I'm left feeling we've really only just touched on the issues — I want to carry on!

It's been good to have this opportunity to talk about the issues, but I do feel that for us to change anything there needs to be a school policy which is initiated by the Management. I also feel there needs to be an *Authority* policy and somebody in the Inspectorate who is responsible for this area. That would make sure that it was taken more seriously.

Obviously a course of this nature is a first step and needs to be followed up, perhaps by a further series of workshops where the original participants can meet to share their progress and problems, or perhaps help to facilitate school-based work. This would require resources from the local education authority.

Summary

As this chapter is written, articles appear daily in the press about the 'increased levels of indiscipline and violence' in our schools. Bullying between children is just one manifestation of this concern. We teachers are often left feeling frustrated and angry as nothing seems to be done and anyway, we don't quite know what to do. The choice sometimes appears to be only between sending the children out of school or doing nothing. We know that the children's behaviour is often a reaction to things beyond our control as teachers — severe emotional problems or an 'acting out' of violence and aggression in society. However, it has been argued here that bullying is partly an outcome of the structure and organisation of schools themselves — where we *do* have power to bring about change.

The teacher in the classroom can make an individual impact and help to foster a sense of respect for others and responsibility for one's own actions. Next, the school needs a policy for a caring ethos and the promotion of such values as respect, caring, tolerance and responsibility for others. Values necessary also for pupils to achieve their full academic potential — no child feels safe in the classroom or can concentrate on learning if bullying goes on. Development of a policy to deal with it must involve the full staff and be on-going. Bullying cannot be dealt with on a purely pastoral level; the pupils may need to change, but so also will the staff and the institution.

Recognising the pervasive nature of bullying in schools and the damage it does to pupils is the first step in working towards its elimination.

References

Archer, J. and Lloyd, B. (1982) *Sex and Gender*. Penguin, Harmondsworth.
Askew, S. and Ross, C. (1988) *Boys Don't Cry*. Open University Press.

Carricoates, K. (1978) 'Dinosaurs in the classroom: a re-examination of some aspects of the hidden curriculum in primary schools, *Women's Studies International Quarterly*, 1 (4), 353-64.

Davison, J. (1985) 'Boys will be . . .?', *The English Curriculum: Gender*, ILEA English Centre.

Newson, J. and Newson, E. (1984) 'Parents' perspectives on children's behaviour at school'. N. Frude and H. Gault (eds.), *Disruptive Behaviour in Schools*, John Wiley.

Nicholson, J. (1984) *Men and Women: How Different Are They?* Oxford University Press.

O'Hagan, F.J. and Edmunds, G. (1982) Pupils' attitudes towards teachers: strategies for controlling disruptive behaviour, *British Journal of Educational Psychology*, 52 (3), November, 331-40.

Olweus, D. (1978) *Aggression in Schools: Bullies and Whipping Boys*, John Wiley.

Smith, C. and Lloyd, B. (1978) 'Maternal behaviour and perceived sex of infant, *Child Development*, 49, 1263-5.

Stanworth, M. (1981) *Gender and Schooling*, Hutchinson.

Tingle, S. (1985), 'Going mixed', *The English Curriculum: Gender*, ILEA English Centre.

Walkerdine, V. (1981), 'Sex, power and pedagogy', *Science Education*, Spring.

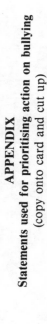

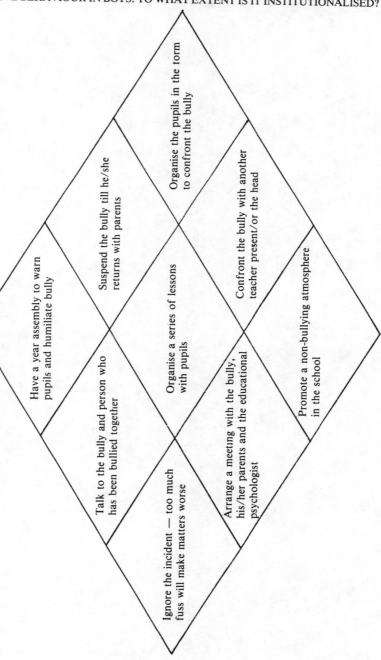

APPENDIX
Statements used for prioritising action on bullying
(copy onto card and cut up)

- Organise the pupils in the form to confront the bully
- Suspend the bully till he/she returns with parents
- Confront the bully with another teacher present/or the head
- Have a year assembly to warn pupils and humiliate bully
- Organise a series of lessons with pupils
- Promote a non-bullying atmosphere in the school
- Talk to the bully and person who has been bullied together
- Arrange a meeting with the bully, his/her parents and the educational psychologist
- Ignore the incident — too much fuss will make matters worse

Chapter 6
A Whole-Curriculum Approach to Bullying
Graham Herbert

School Background

The school is an 11-16 mixed comprehensive with some 1200 pupils on roll. A Secondary Modern and a Girls Grammar School were combined in the early seventies. The catchment area is mainly private housing with some rented accommodation. As the school expanded, care was taken to maintain public credibility by heavy investment in achieving academic success. Consequently, a two-banded system developed, with the upper band following a traditional academic curriculum, and the lower a more practical and, we hoped, relevant curriculum. This was regularly modified to meet changing pupils' needs, national and local governmental initiatives, and the shifting patterns of employment.

As the school roll began to fall from its height of 1500, pressure was exerted on the curriculum. Differing structures and models have been investigated but the upper banding persists, albeit in changed and more flexible form. Many of the disaffected, bullying pupils are to be found in the lower band, however, and some at the bottom of the upper band. Although generalisations about bullying can be deceptive about individual circumstances, in this school bullying has clearly become a way of achieving status, an alternative to the norm of academic success.

Some years ago, a particular group of lower ability pupils began to exhibit unpleasant bullying tendencies. The boys were mostly aggressive and physically threatening. They would intimidate weaker or less confident pupils into providing them with treats such as sweets or cigarettes or sometimes money. The victim's school equipment would be hidden or scattered around playing fields, perhaps his homework destroyed. Sometimes the victim would be followed around school, so denied a hiding place. If the victim retaliated in an way, he was ridiculed and physically threatened. Only rarely was the victim hit. The bullies relied on the victim's fear of being hit, and the knowledge that he was incapable of defending himself.

The girls were less physically threatening, although the same 'treats' were expected. A victim would be isolated by a group of erstwhile friends and acquaintances. The girls would have a pact not to speak to one of their number, or sit next to her in lessons, as though she were unclean or smelled. The bullies would ridicule just the things of which young girls are acutely conscious: their developing figures, their clothes, their general appearance, their attempts at make-up. On one occasion a girl's sexual behaviour was ridiculed; she was accused of being 'common', a 'slag', of having a venereal disease. Graffitti appeared on the toilet walls condemning her and her supposed boyfriends. The poor girl was made a social pariah. In such cases the problem is not the fear of physical violence but the constant condemnation, isolation and loneliness. Victims of such social manipulation generally accuse the ringleader of 'taking my friends away from me'.

Investigating the problem, the Head of Year concluded that defining the nature of bullying was difficult and that it was more widespread than was realised. If a pupil felt intimidated on more than one occasion by a pupil or group of pupils, this was defined as bullying. Much of what was perceived by pupils as bullying could not possibly be detected by staff: some pupils, for example, feared using the toilets. The distress and anxiety this caused, particularly to pubescent girls, can be imagined but not detected. With a working definition and greater awareness of the problem, the Head of Year sought to tackle bullying via the curriculum.

This approach may appear strange and at first it was questioned and its likely efficacy doubted. One of the original arguments for developing tutorial or pastoral time was to overcome such social problems. The Head of Year argued that the fear and misery induced on victims did not vanish with the end of tutorial time, but carried on into Maths or Science or Games. Worse still were the unsupervised movements between lessons. The mid-morning break and the lunchhour are highlights of the school day, time to socialise, have fun, play games. For some pupils, however, it is a time of hiding, of fear, of dread. If there is bullying then, for the victim it shapes the day and is a constant worry. To remove fear induced by bullying, we must tackle it all day long. Pastoral work on its own is not enough.

Initial Work

The English Department had adopted Barnes' models of classroom interaction (1978, 1981) and pupils were used to working in small groups. This was particularly useful for the group of pupils causing the concern. The Head of Year was also a member of the English Department; the timetable was changed so that the target group of pupils — both victims and bullies — was in the same English group, following a course of continuous assessment.

Working in small groups encourages pupils to use their own language, formulate their own ideas, collaborate with each other, speculate and hypothesise. Importantly, it allows pupils to express their point of view. This lessens the feelings of inadequacy victims often have and may positively develop self-esteem. Victims are often unwilling to approach a teacher, or any adult, for help. It breaks a pupil code, so risks incurring further victimisation. Teachers are powerless to act in this situation, even though they are aware of the problem. Working in small groups in the classroom, however, pupils can critically examine their assumptions and beliefs, air their opinions and express their feelings. Crucially, this is triggered, not by someone whose views they would tend to reject as a matter of course, but by their peers.

Something was clearly amiss. There had been complaints by both staff and pupils, about pupils' behaviour and their attitudes to each other. Much of the bullying was directed at weaker members of the peer group rather than younger children in the school. One attempt to reduce the effects of bullying on the victims was to work in the English lessons on a novel which presented bullying from the victim's point of view. The book chosen was *There is a Happy Land* by Keith

Waterhouse, which explores feelings of isolation experienced by young people. Other novels that would be suitable are the popular *Buddy* and, for older pupils, *Lord of the Flies* or *Roll of Thunder, Hear My Cry,* which also raises issues of racism.

Alongside this curriculum approach, a long-term pastoral approach aimed to reduce the effects of bullying on the victims. Each case of bullying was treated individually by the Head of Year, the Deputy Head, and the parents, as appropriate. But referring bullies to authority figures can only be a short-term solution. Punitive measures adopted against bullies can be perceived as intimidating, or 'bullying' the bullies. A disciplinary reaction by the school can create tightly-knit sub-cultures of intimidators which are merely reinforced by any attempts to break them down. However, having identified these groups, it was possible to determine what behaviour displayed by the victim induced the bullying. The victim could then be helped to alter behaviour patterns to lessen the likelihood of being bullied.

Separate groups within the class were given specific problems to discuss in terms of both the novel and their own experiences. The pupils were asked to recall their own observations and to relate them to the feelings expressed in the novel. At first the pupils found it difficult to relate their personal feelings, but with encouragement they were able to express themselves cogently. Each group then elected a spokesperson to report to the class. Each group consisted of known bullies and known and regular victims, so each was aware of both sides of the problem. Each group was single-sex so reflecting the differing forms of bullying: physical threats and social manipulation. As each spokesperson delivered his or her group's findings, summaries were written up on the blackboard and common elements highlighted. What emerged from the boys was a feeling of camaraderie — in fact the bullying was an attempt to promote this feeling, to knit the group together. The typical victim was one who tried to infiltrate the group and become accepted, to gain status by association. The victim generally tried to buy acceptance, using a variety of techniques — offering bribes in the form of sweets, cigarettes or services in the form of completed homework, or inside information in the form of gossip. These tactics worked only in the short term, but incurred further bullying in the long run. The victim was not related to, nor perceived as an individual. From the boys' group emerged a pattern of physical threats, from the girls a pattern of rejection, of complete isolation from erstwhile friends. When questioned about such behaviour, victims claimed, 'I thought they were my friends', or 'We were all going round together'. A bully would make a generalisation, 'He's a wally', or 'He's a fairy. We put up with him because we felt sorry for him, but he became a pest'.

The groups were then re-formed and a different question posed: how can one avoid becoming a victim? The pupils could make deductions from information on the board, which they had compiled themselves. All groups gave similar answers. The boys argued that they should not try to infiltrate sub-groups but should develop a worthwhile relationship with another individual. The girls argued a similar case; a meaningful relationship with another individual meant that, no matter how the group behaved, individuals were never isolated. Thus, rather than the condemnation of a group and its sub-culture by an authority figure, which would serve to reinforce the group, it was possible to outline strategies that victims and potential victims could adopt to avoid being perceived as such. Consequently the victim could help himself and improve his self-esteem — thereby lessening the likelihood of being bullied.

The pupils used their work to complete two pieces of work for their English assignments. One was an imaginative response to the literature; the other a literary response. In her imaginative essay, one fifteen year-old expressed ideas echoed by other girls and boys in the class:

> It's good to have a best friend because you can have a laugh doing nothing. If you're miserable she'll cheer you up and won't mind. You can trust her, tell her your secrets and know she won't make you look a fool.

Further Developments

This approach had a limited, though significant, effect on a small number of pupils. However, it had no effect on pupils not being taught by the Head of Year; nor any impact on pupils in other years. The classic dilemma still operated: any attempts at breaking down a knot of bullies by figures in authority resulted in a tightening of the knot.

Bullying as a topic was considered by all pupils in their form. Each year group considered bullying as a topic in their form tutorials and examined the ways it affected them at each stage as they progressed through the school. There are plenty of materials: video programmes, tutorial handbooks and books on personal and social education. However tackling the problem solely through the pastoral curriculum can allow it to be passed over as someone else's problem. If bullying is viewed as a 'pastoral problem' the issue can be easily bureaucratized. When asked how the school combats bullying, there are obvious schemes of work, monitoring of incidents and so on to show. None of this shows the *victim* that the school is a caring place; nor does it reassure parents. The caring ethos must be made explicit through the curriculum and the daily dealings with individuals. If the strategies to deal with bullying are compartmentalised, they will lack credibility with pupils and staff.

There was no reliable data available on the nature or the extent of bullying in other years in the school. A questionnaire had been developed by an Educational Psychologist in the authority in conjunction with another secondary school and this provided relatively reliable data. But it was decided that information from this survey might be 'politically' sensitive if it fell into 'the wrong hands'. Despite some arguments in favour of running the questionnaire it was finally rejected. Nevertheless, staff attention had been focused onto the subject and the debate itself had heightened awareness across the entire staff. Such an awareness meant that bullying could be discussed as a topic in lessons other than English. The topic arose as a natural extension to many areas of Modern History — the rise of Fascism, Civil Rights in America and so on. The topic also arose in certain Geography lessons. By extending the discussion of bullying beyond an individual lesson, the school's stance on bullying became embedded in the ethos of the school. We are now looking for ways of rewarding those form groups for which no instances of bullying are recorded. It is hoped that this will bring communal pressure to bear upon individual, would-be bullies to conform to the group norm, rather than seeking status from this unpleasant deviance.

Outside Agencies

Once awareness of the difficult nature of bullying had been developed in all staff and the school's stance against it made explicit through the curriculum, it was time for known victims to be given extra support. Help was enlisted from the Education Social Worker (ESW) and other support agencies to set up a small social skills group. Social skills training was not part of the regular school curriculum. Certain pupils, because of their emotional needs and lack of appropriate skills, failed to use fully the opportunities the school offered. Social skills training was one way of meeting those needs and of demonstrating the value of such a course in a flexible curriculum.

Eight known victims of bullying formed a group — those whose parents had become known to the Head of Year plus those whom other staff, as well as the Head of Year, had identified as being at risk. They generally lacked confidence and some had truanted and were already known to the ESW.

The aims of the group were:

1. to help participants develop an awareness of what happens in social situations and to provide practice in the skills needed to cope effectively;
2. to heighten the self-esteem of group members by providing opportunities to improve their relationships with others;
3. to encourage pupils to formulate positive goals.

Parental consent was enlisted. Parents had been made aware of the distress caused in their children by the bullies; co-operation in the venture was seen as a positive way of helping the individuals. Sessions were planned with a variety of activities including:

Trust games to foster an environment of trust.
Brainstorming to identify areas of concern.
Cartooning to identify concerns.
Role play to model alternative ways of handling problem situations.
Mime to illustrate methods of non-verbal communication.
Group discussion.
Assessment scales and questionnaires to provide profiles of problem areas and to help in the setting of objectives.

A careful plan was drawn up prior to each session; and each session was evaluated afterwards by the group leaders. We tended to put too much into the hourly session, but this was felt preferable to too little. Should one idea not work, there was always something else to try. Each session had a general aim combined with observable student outcomes. Thus session one was written as follows:

1. *warm-up games: famous people*
    materials: card, sellotape, marker pen
    aim: mixing, starting conversation, ice-breaking
    objectives: students will participate in the game, accept the rules of the game
                and hopefully enjoy themselves.

Names of famous people are written on a piece of stiff card and one fastened
to the back of each individual. By asking questions of each other, each participant has to work out the name of the celebrity pinned to his back. This
can be great fun and encourages shy, retiring pupils to ask questions of
others.

2. *warm-up games: killer-wink*
    materials: a pack of cards
    aim: establish eye contact
    objectives: as above.

As many cards are taken out of a pack as there are members in the group,
including group leaders. Only one of the cards is a picture. The cards are
dealt out and players secretly note their card before handing them back. The
player who received the picture is the 'murderer' and must wink at another
player to 'kill' him. The 'body' states that he has been 'killed' and takes
no further part in the game. This continues until all the group has been
'assassinated' or until someone spots the murderer 'committing his crime'.
He is then challenged and the game begins again. This, too, is fun and encourages the retiring individuals to look at other people at the same time
as tolerating the gaze of others.

3. *brainstorming: 1001 uses of a shoe*
    materials: none
    aim: to introduce idea of brainstorming
    objectives: students will generate ideas quickly, students will think creatively,
                students will collaborate.

4. *self-assessment: questionnaire* (see Bond, 1986)
    materials: self-assessment sheet (developed by group leaders), pencils
    aim: to provide profiles of problem areas
    objectives: students will complete a self-assessment survey, by patterns which
                relate to them as individuals.

5. *concluding game: watchtower*
    materials: blindfolds
    aim: to practice listening skills, to develop trust
    objectives: as for other games

One player is shown an obstacle course made out of tables, chairs and the
like, which he must negotiate blindfolded. He is blindfolded, disorientated

by spinning, then given instructions by another group member, to whom he must listen carefully and trust implicitly. No contact is allowed between players. Once again this is fun and group members must trust each other, knowng that their trust is not betrayed.

A further nine sessions were prepared, the games becoming more complicated and their relation to social skills being made more explicit as time went by (Bond, 1986). They covered a variety of skills: listening, holding conversations, asking for help, dealing with feelings, negotiating, responding to teasing, dealing with contradictory messages, prioritising and so on (Corfield and Wells, 1976; Brandes and Ginnis, 1986). The sessions took place after school and were well attended — to the surprise of the cynics on the staff who had scoffed at the idea.

A short discussion followed each session, guided by the group leaders, highlighting the social aims of the session and how social skills could be taught and learned. Pupils were encouraged to say what they had learned and were invariably positive and supportive. Statements such as, 'Today I learned how helpful Joanne is', or 'Today I learned what fun teachers can be', were common.

Such feedback acted as the first form of evaluation for the group leaders. Further evaluation was carried out, albeit subjectively, amongst group leaders the following day. Opinions were sought from subject teachers and the pupils' absence rates, truancy rates and rate of referral to the Head of Year were carefully monitored. Such illuminative evaluation benefitted the staff, who felt they were receiving some support with difficult pupils; it also benefitted pupils who came to think of the school as a safe place.

Significantly, known bullies were excluded from the group. One particularly active bully pleaded to be included in a group and was told she could join in another group at a later stage. She began to take an active interest in school work, commiting herself to working on her own at dinner times. Staff commented on the change in her and how positive her attitude had become. The social isolation of the bully had worked far more effectively than authoritative attempts to stop her.

Through sessions like these it was hoped to give the most vulnerable members of the school community the ability to cope with potential bullies. It also acted as an addition to and support of what was happening in lessons and the ethos of the school generally.

Summary

Dealing with bullying in this way is not straightforward for it reveals politically sensitive information that could be exploited by the unscrupulous. It must be stressed to pupils, parents and staff that the school takes seriously the distress caused by bullying and will adopt strategies to combat it. Each incident is dealt with separately. The co-operation of parents is a pre-condition. The curriculum has to be flexible enough to change quickly, according to circumstances. Victims need all the support they can be given to help them become socially skilled and avoid being perceived as victims. Perhaps the most important factor in combating bullying is the social pressure brought to bear by the peer group rather than the condemnation of individual bullies by someone in authority.

References

Barnes, D. (1976). *From Communication to Curriculum*. Penguin.

Barnes, D. (1982). *Practical Curriculum Study*. Routledge and Kegan Paul.

Bond, T. (1986). *Games for Social and Life Skills*. Hutchinson.

Cerfield, J., and Wells, H.C. (1976). *100 Ways to Enhance Self-Concept in the Classroom*. Prentice-Hall, New Jersey.

Brandes, D., and Ginnis, P. (1986). *A Guide to Student-Centred Learning*. Basil Blackwell.

Chapter 7
Bullying in Public Schools: Myth and Reality
Geoffrey Walford

'Very well then, let's roast him', cried Flashman, and catches hold of Tom by the collar: one or two boys hesitate, but the rest join in. East seizes Tom's arm and tries to pull him away, but is knocked back by one of the boys, and Tom is dragged along struggling. His shoulders are pushed against the mantelpiece, and he is held by main force before the fire, Flashman drawing his trousers tight by way of extra torture . . .

'Will you sell now for ten shillings?' says one boy who is relenting.

Tom only answers by groans and struggles. 'I say, Flashy, he has had enough', says the same boy, dropping the arm he holds.

'No, no, another turn'll do it', answers Flashman.

But poor Tom is done already, turns deadly pale, and his head falls forward on his breast . . .

(Hughes, 1857)

In *Tom Brown's Schooldays* Thomas Hughes recounts a vivid scene of Tom being bullied by older boys. Flashman has forced every boy in the house to enter a sweepstake for the Derby. Tom draws the favourite and refuses to sell his ticket back to the fifth year bullies. Tom thus undergoes a painful and sadistic roasting in front of an open fire in an attempt to persuade him of the wisdom of accepting Flashman's five shilling offer for the ticket.

This fictional account is an extreme example of the bullying that many people still associate with life in the public boarding schools, where young boys are at the mercy of older boys within an unjust and tyrannical system. In this chapter I hope to show that, while many such schools were rough and lawless institutions in the past, the present day reality is rather different.

Historical Background

The independent secondary sector of schooling in Britain is marked by its diversity, ranging from small, co-educational day schools serving a local clientele which may have been established only in the last few years, to major single sex boarding schools which can trace their history back through many centuries. In contrast to the popular image, the majority of pupils in independent secondary schools are day pupils whose experiences differ little from those of similar pupils in many state maintained selective schools. In this chapter, however, I wish to consider the so called 'public' schools. While there is no totally accepted definition, it is generally accepted that those schools whose headmaster is a member of the Headmasters' Conference have a right to call themselves 'public school' if they wish to do so. Within this group I wish to discuss the 50 or so boarding schools, of ancient Victorian foundation, which were until recently for boys only. Included within this group are Charterhouse, Cheltenham and Clifton; Radley, Repton and Rugby; Wellington, Winchester and Westminster. In short — schools 'something like Rugby'.

Rugby of course, was the school depicted by Thomas Hughes in *Tom Brown's Schooldays*. That somewhat idealised account, where good ultimately triumphs over evil, was written in the 1850s about the school as it was at the time of Thomas Arnold some twenty years earlier. But the roasting is based on fact, for there is a great deal of evidence that such gross bullying had been prevalent in most of the public schools since their foundation and had continued throughout the Victorian era. The sheer brutality of public school life is a constant theme in the many histories of the system. Chandos (1984), for example, catalogues some of the initiation rites which boys had to endure in the nineteenth century — running the gauntlet at Winchester, being tossed in a blanket at the ceiling at Eton, hands being seared with burning wood at Winchester, or being forced to drink a jug of muddy water crammed with salt at Rugby. Similarly, Gathorne-Hardy (1977) documents cases of roasting before a fire, and of being shut in a trunk with sawdust until nearly suffocated at Charterhouse. Boys were sometimes left permanently injured, and occasionally even died, as a result of such treatment.

Although these initiation rites were perhaps the worst examples of ritualised sadism, bullying and violence were an integral part of the public school system. Housemasters usually ran houses for their own private profit. They largely left the boys to organise themselves, and helped to institutionalise bullying through a system of prefects and fagging. There are accounts of fagging, dating from the mid-seventeenth century, in which a young boy might find himself the virtual slave of an older boy. Older boys forced those younger and weaker than themselves to perform a multitude of menial tasks for them and, if they failed to do them to satisfaction, were allowed to beat and abuse them. Gathorne-Hardy (1977) quotes the following example of fagging at Eton in 1824:

> The condition of a junior colleger's life at that period was very hard indeed. The practice of fagging had become an organised system of brutality, and cruelty. I was frequently kept up until one or two o'clock in the morning, waiting on my masters at upper and indulging every sort of bullying at their hands. I have been beaten on my palms with the back of a brush, or struck on both sides of my face, because I had not closed the shutter near my master's bed tight enough or because in making his bed I had left the seam of the lower sheet uppermost.

Within the prefect system bullying was legitimated as part of a wider system of corporal punishment. For not only did young boys suffer at the hands of older boys, they also frequently lived in fear of masters and headmaster. As Honey (1977) points out, the use of corporal punishment was part of the fabric of nineteenth-century English education, not just in the public schools but in all other types of schools as well. 'The birch was part of the standard equipment of the Victorian schoolmaster, as central to the work of teaching as is the

82

textbook or the blackboard of today'. Flogging, using the birch or similar, was a widely accepted part of schooling. Some of the worst examples of the flogging masters and headmasters have almost become folk devils as a result of their sadistic exploits. For example, Moss of Shrewsbury is said to have once given a boy eighty-eight strokes. At Eton, Warre had an elaborate ritual involving two 'holders-down', two prefects and the headmaster's clerk. Keate, also at Eton, once publicly birched over 100 boys for rushing to their places in Chapel at the last moment (Griggs, 1985). In such a climate, there is little wonder that boys also did violence to those younger than themselves.

The worst excesses of violence by masters and prefects were gradually curbed throughout the first half of this century, but Kalton's (1966) survey of the public schools showed that in 1964 some two-thirds of the schools with boarders still allowed some boys to administer corporal punishment. Four-fifths of the fully boarding schools allowed it, and in some of these schools the right was widespread. A fagging system of the type where young boys did menial tasks for older boys was still in operation in more than half of the schools.

John Rae (1981), former headmaster of Westminster School, argues that it was not until the 1960s and the 1970s that the public schools underwent dramatic change. In the 1960s the 'teenage revolution' meant that boys were less willing to exercise power over others. As they questioned the authority of the masters and other adults, they began to refuse positions of authority themselves. The prefect system became less important in the running of the schools and houses, and masters began to take a larger part in the everyday organisation of the schools. This lead to a decrease in both authorised and unauthorised violence. There were other changes, too. Parents became much more closely involved with the schools and demanded higher standards of care for their children. Parents and boys wanted better physical accommodation, smaller dormitories and more privacy. Houses were thus altered or rebuilt to give study rooms and bedrooms for the older boys, which meant that the younger boys were less open to abuse. Relationships between boys of different ages softened and became less hierarchical. The 1970s brought further changes, as pupils in public schools increasingly felt the need to obtain good academic qualifications. Entry to universities and future careers now depended on A level passes, and schools became more academically selective in their intakes. Many of the roughest were excluded. The importance of sport declined, and with it went even more of the 'roughness and toughness' of the schools. Physical prowess was no longer particularly desirable.

A further important change which has occurred since the 1960s is the introduction of girls into these previously male-only preserves. John Rae (1981) recounts:

In the early sixties no public school was co-educational. There were independent co-educational schools, the best kown of which was Bedales, but it was precisely because such schools admitted girls as well as boys that they were regarded as not public schools but as experimental and outside the main tradition.

By 1980 about 100 of the 210 Headmasters' Conference schools admitted girls either at the sixth form or throughout. By 1984 the majority of HMC schools admitted girls, although about 70 of these were for the sixth form only. Whatever the original reasons for opening the schools to girls (I have discussed some possibilities in Walford, 1986), they have had a considerable impact on the atmosphere of the schools. There is a continuing debate about the behavioural and attitudinal effects of co-education on both boys and girls, and it can be argued that the effects on girls are not always beneficial (Deem, 1984). Nevertheless, it is clear that boys usually benefit from an increased academic emphasis and a decrease in the aggressive masculinity which is endemic in many boys' schools. While girls do sometimes bully other girls, the general picture is that their influence on the degree of acceptability of violence is almost wholly beneficial.

The Extent of Change

Without doubt, the ritualised and legitimised violence of the Victorian era has now disappeared. But the question remains as to whether some forms of bullying persist in the schools. Understandably, unambiguous evidence on the topic of bullying is very difficult to find. The existence and extent of bullying is hardly the sort of information which schools are likely to include in their prospectuses! The competitive situation in which schools find themselves means that writers from within the schools are likely to play down any problems, and it is rare for outside researchers to be given the chance to find out. However, such a chance occurred for me early in the 1980s while I was conducting an ethnographic study of public school life, and the data and argument presented in this section are based upon that study, conducted in two of the major public boarding schools in England. About a month was spent in one school and a whole term in the other. The first school was for boys only, the second was for boys in the junior forms but with a co-educational sixth form. Interviews were conducted with teaching, administrative and domestic staff as well as pupils, and time was spent observing lessons, meetings, sports and both formal and informal social occasions. More details of the research methods and substantive findings have been published elsewhere (Walford, 1984; 1986 a and b: 1987).

Data was also obtained from a questionnaire which was given to about 200 pupils in the second of the research schools. The questionnaire used was a shortened version of that used by Lambert *et al.* in their studies of boarding schools (Lambert and Millham, 1968; Lambert, Bullock and Millham, 1970; Lambert 1975). It was completed by practically all of the first and second year boys at the school (i.e. 13-15 year olds) in class time, in class groups. As described elsewhere (Walford, 1986a), the boys generally welcomed the chance to tell someone what they thought, and treated the questions seriously — only 2 per cent of the questionnaires had to be discarded because of facetious responses. Not every question was answered by every boy, but the lowest reponse rate was 90 per cent.

The questionnaire did not ask any direct questions on bullying or violence, and neither word appeared in any of the questions. The data discussed here were obtained from two questions: (1) 'Life anywhere gives us all problems. What are the most important personal problems *for you* which are caused mainly by life here?' and (2) 'What are the things you most dislike about being here? *Say why.*'

Before considering the answers mentioning violence or bullying, it is worth examining the other sorts of problems which these boys experienced. The range was considerable. Some points were made by just one boy, such as: 'uncomfortable beds', 'getting up at 7.15 a.m.', 'Saturday morning classes' and even 'the independence is too much for me'. Other problems were mentioned by several boys and included: 'money', 'being thought to be a snob by state school pupils', 'Housemaster' and 'masters'. Specific masters were sometimes named. Some of the more frequent problem areas were illustrated by comments such as: 'work — I can't do it well', 'exams', 'lack of contact with the outside world', 'depression', 'lack of privacy', 'bad food' or 'not enough food' and 'lack of girls'. By the fourth year, in particular, the complaint about the lack of girls of their own age was very frequent indeed. However, another common comment was on the lines of 'I don't have any problems at all' or 'I like it here all the time'.

This last comment was backed by evidence from another question where, overall, 74 per cent of the boys said that they either thoroughly enjoyed being at the school or had a reasonably pleasant time at the school. Only six per cent claimed to be unhappy. Without quite mentioning bullying some of the boys in the wider group indicated that personal relationships were a problem. For example, 'getting on with people I don't like', 'the few nasty people there are here' and 'constant arguments with people' were a problem to some of the boys.

More seriously, in all, more than 10 per cent of the boys mentioned bullying, violence or being teased in answer to one or both of these two questions. As might be expected, there were more comments on bullying from the third year boys than from the fourth year boys. All of the relevant comments from these third year boys are given below, with an indication of which question led to the response.

101 (2) The fags are often bullied by 'power crazy' study holders, and that can upset weak minded people immensely.

102 (1) being pushed around by seniors.
(2) older boys who push you around.

107 (1) bullying.
(2) the boys in my house, in my year, because I don't get on with them.

114 (1) There are people who make life unpleasant for you. Older unpleasant boys like to make you look a fool. This no longer happens to me, but it used to.

120 (2) Teased, picked on.

121 (2) I dislike the bullying, stamping on, grouping up or cling-ons (those who cling to the big guys).

136 (2) Being pushed around by older boys with authority. Being given punishments by them because they're sadists.

150 (1) You find that sometimes 'gangs' of people join together and get at you, and then another person, and so it goes on.

155 (1) Being bullied was my problem here. Even the people in my own year tease me and bully me, and there is nothing I can do about it yet.

168 (1) People are very aggressive and don't understand you. The upper years forget what it is like to be at the bottom.

174 (1) I occasionally am teased and bullied by some boys because I am eccentric and badly coordinated.
(2) I was bullied at first because I was eccentric.

186 (1) bullying.

188 (2) some boys are bullies and push their weight around.

While it is possible to quibble about whether or not some of these comments are strong enough to be labelled bullying, and, of course, it is difficult to test the validity of the replies, these comments are a cause for concern and deserve to be treated seriously. I observed some boys being bullied during my period of research, but I was actually surprised at the number of boys who wrote about bullying in their questionnaires. Further, as these two questions did not explicitly ask about bullying or violence, it is likely that the full extent of general concern about the matter is not revealed.

In the second year there were slightly fewer complaints of this nature, but they were still far from being uncommon.

206 (1) People often tease and joke about my bottom lip which is larger than my upper lip and I hate it when it happens.

207 (1) People seem to enjoy rotting up others and especially when one starts up the others join in to attack (either words or fists) the same person, often weaker than those attacking them.
(2) bullying. I am a victim.

213 (1) I find that I am sometimes 'victimised', but it does not really bother me.

217 (1) The main problem is to stop myself being teased too much.
(2) big groups of people gang together and victimise certain others.

226 (1) People more senior to you can be unpleasant to you and you can't do anything about it.

261 (1) Well, as I am a foreigner, some people tend to look down on me. I am always conscious of my nationality and the colour of my skin and I feel a bit angry when others are making a joke about this.
(2) Some of the people here are not pleasant at all and are really hard to get on with.

264 (2) The sixth form bullies.

It must be remembered that these comments come from just one of the major public boarding schools, but there is no reason to believe that the school is atypical. Further, an analysis of the questionnaires showed that the problem was not restricted to one or two of the houses, but that every house in the school had at least one boy who complained.

While I was at the schools I also observed some of this bullying going on. For example, in *Life in Public Schools* (Walford, 1986a) I gave an account of the bullying of a boy I called Paul. He was a small, frail boy with traces of a slight physical disability. His family was affluent and secure, but his world at school was one of insecurity and isolation. I would see him wandering around the school alone, receiving jeers and the occasional mild physical assault. In his case the tormentors were his peers rather than older boys, but the relentless teasing was still in the end more than he could take, and he was removed from the school by his parents.

Such an extreme case is unusual, but it is typical in the way that bullying in these schools is no longer a matter of gross physical abuse, but is a mixture of constant teasing and mild violence. I talked about bullying with some masters and boys in the school, and it was very clear that any visible physical abuse of younger boys by older boys, or their stronger peers, would be very heavily punished by the housemasters or masters — probably involving the threat or actual expulsion of the perpetrator. Bullying is now a matter of verbal and light physical abuse rather than heavy physical oppression. For some boys, however, the effects may still cause considerable harm. At the very least, such behaviour leads to much unhappiness for the victims.

Conclusion

The other papers in this volume show that, unfortunately, bullying is still an everyday feature of life in most schools. It would seem that in any group of several hundred young people there are bound to be some who delight in tormenting and physically abusing those younger or weaker than themselves. Adolescence is a time of personal uncertainty and self-doubt, which can often be translated into particularly antisocial behaviour.

It is tempting to try to draw comparisons between the nature and extent of bullying in these public boarding schools and that in some state maintained schools. Such comparisons are very difficult to make and to have any meaning at all would have to take into account the social class compositions of the schools and the marital and family backgrounds of particular groups involved. However, the very firm sanctions imposed by public schools against the most obvious forms of bullying make it likely that the level of physical violence in such schools is generally lower. Nevertheless, it has been shown that there is a worryingly high number of pupils who experience what they define as bullying within these schools. They would appear to classify somewhat lower levels of abuse within the term 'bullying'. Thus, activities which might be defined as 'teasing' in another school would seem to be often described as 'bullying' here.

Such distinctions in the way in which activities are perceived should not be ignored, for the different circumstances in which boys find themselves lead them to interpret their experience in a different way. The pain they feel is real. The main difference, of course, is that in a boarding school there is no respite. If a boy is the subject of teasing or mild physical abuse in a day school he is still able to get away from it for most of the day, simply because he goes home and leaves his tormentors behind. A secure family home can, to an extent, protect the boy from the worst threats to self-identity and self-esteem. In a boarding school there is no escape. The family is physically and mentally too far away to have much effect on what is sometimes a daily and continuous assault on the growing person. The bullies of the public boarding schools do not have to indulge in gross violent behaviour to cause harm. Their activities might even be defined as 'joking' in another context, but in a closed environment, where just a few specific boys become picked out to receive such mild abuse, it becomes 'bullying'. Boys use the term 'bullying' because that is what it feels like to them at the receiving end.

Headmasters and staff of public boarding schools would generally appear to take overt bullying seriously and to make sure that any transgressions are firmly dealt with. In terms of the degree of actual assault involved, the schools are probably far less violent than most other schools. However, the data gathered from pupils indicate that staff need to be even more careful than they are now. They need to take seriously the way in which pupils interpret the actions of other pupils and to attempt to prohibit all forms of covert as well as overt bullying.

References

Chandos, J. (1984). *Boys Together. English Public Schools 1800-1864,* Hutchinson.
Deem, R. (1984) (Ed.). *Co-Education Reconsidered,* Open University Press.
Gathorne-Hardy, J. (1977). *The Public School Phenomenon,* Hodder and Stoughton.
Griggs, C. (1985). *Private Schools in Britain,* Falmer.
Honey, J.R. de S. (1977). *Tom Brown's Universe. The development of the Public School in the 19th century,* Millington.
Hughes, T. (1857). *Tom Brown's Schooldays,* Macmillan.
Kalton, G. (1966). *The Public Schools: A Factual Survey,* Longmans.
Lambert, R. (1975). *The Chance of a Lifetime?,* Weidenfeld and Nicolson.
Lambert, R., Bullock, R., and Millham, S. (1970). *A Manual to the Sociology of the School,* Weidenfeld and Nicolson.
Lambert, R., and Millham, S. (1968). *The Hothouse Society,* Weidenfeld and Nicolson.
Rae, J. (1981). *The Public School Revolution,* Faber.
Walford, G. (1984). 'The changing professionalism of public school teachers', in *British Public Schools: Policy and Practice* (Ed. G. Walford), pp.111-135, Falmer.
Walford, G. (1986a). *Life in Public Schools,* Methuen.
Walford, G. (1986b). 'Ruling-class classification and framing', *British Educational Research Journal,* 12, 2, 183-195.
Walford, G. (1987). 'Research role conflicts and compromises in public schools', in *Doing Sociology of Education* (Ed. G. Walford), pp.45-65, Falmer.

Chapter 8
Bullying and Persistent School Absenteeism
Ken Reid

The precise relationship between bullying and truancy and school absenteeism is not known. One of my own studies found that bullying was the initial reason given by fifteen per cent of a sample of persistent absentees for first missing school. The same group indicated that it is one of the major reasons for their continued absence from school in nineteen per cent of cases. In this study, bullying was one of six institutional categories isolated from information gleaned from regular interviews with 128 persistent school absentees and two matching control groups (Reid, 1983a).

Of course, no firm conclusions should be drawn from this evidence for a number of reasons. First, the findings were unique to the study. The schools, for example, were situated in a deprived, inner-city region in South Wales. Second, bullying was perceived by the pupils as a major and disproportionate problem in one of the two schools and was rarely mentioned in the other. Third, it is probable that specific percentages would vary in follow-up studies, even those conducted in the same locations.

Therefore, at best, the conclusion that there is a relationship between bullying and school absenteeism indicates a trend rather than a definitive 'causal' relationship. Accordingly, the remainder of this chapter will speculate on reasons why the relationship between perceived and actual bullying and school absenteeism might be particularly significant to this category of deviant pupils. To assist me in my hypothetical analysis, I will lean heavily on my own research experience of work with groups of problem pupils like absentees as well as my own practical and managerial experience in schools (Reid, 1985; 1986a; 1987a,b; Reid et al., 1987).

Research findings demonstrate that persistent school absentees tend to have lower levels of academic and general self-esteem than the normal population (Reid, 1982). Moreover, they are more likely to come from low social class backgrounds and to be brought up in larger families, in poorer housing, in low income families and amongst families who are deprived in a number of other ways. They are also more likely to have come from broken homes or split family situations (Reid, 1986b).

Thus, many persistent school absentees are nurtured on a diet of squabbles and deprivation at home and repeated failure at school. The latter situation is exacerbated by the fact that school absentees tend to have below average levels of intelligence, attainment and interest in their school or school work. Some also tend to be isolates and to have fewer friends in school and in their neighbourhoods than their peers.

It should not be considered surprising therefore, that so many absentees have low self-concepts. But it is precisely because of their lower levels of self-esteem that they are unable to cope with threatening or unusual situations which occur in schools. Whilst one of their more ebullient classmates can laugh off a threat from a peer, many introverted absentees cannot. Rather, they brood and dwell on the threat and often withdraw from the threatening stimuli.

Indeed, in some cases, absentees make the 'threat' seem greater than it really is. For instance, in my sample of persistent absentees, one boy first began to miss school because his classmates 'kept pinching my soccer cards and throwing them away'. Later, the same pupil stayed away because he refused to (or couldn't) pay two pence a day 'protection money' to older pupils in the playground. At the beginning the pupil could have solved his own problems. No doubt every other pupil in his class had already done so when challenged, but he was unable to. Later, he was identified as a 'soft touch' by his classmates — almost pitifully helpless. In other words, his peers recognised his weakness. Similar traits are apparent in pupils who stay away from school because they are teased, made fun of or called names.

Clearly therefore, to absentees, acts of bullying can be major or minor, real or imagined. What is important to them is that a threat has been made. Once the threat is made, their defence mechanisms leave them more vulnerable than many of their peers, reinforced by their lower levels of self-esteem, social, familial and educational circumstances.

This leads to a related point. There is in the literature and amongst teachers, parents and professionals, a tendency to think of bullying as being mainly physical. It is not. The mental pain is often at least as great as the physical. Furthermore, it is rare for physical bullying to take place without an associated mental problem.

Similarly, while physical bullying can often be spotted easily, certainly upon medical examination, it is frequently hard, even impossible, to discern pure mental bullying. When is it real? When is it imagined? When is it embellishment, or pure fiction? Quite often, teachers and parents understandably have little or no idea that a child is suffering mental anguish — whether for realistic or unrealistic reasons.

Sometimes, too, there can be a blurring between physical and mental reality. In my study, John claimed to be being victimised by his PE teacher. He said it was because he did not have a proper soccer kit. Nevertheless, he was made to play football. When he did, he claimed people didn't tackle him but they kicked him instead. So he started missing every games lesson including swimming.

The simple truth is that the mental anguish which some children suffer at school makes it difficult to be certain when their psychological fears are rational or irrational — true or imaginary. Explicitly, a pupil can have a fear of walking into a crowded room with her peers. The basis of her fear lies perhaps in earlier 'mocking' or teasing about her appearance. Perhaps it is because she feels self-conscious about her own appearance and does not realise that her looks are of little importance to her peers. Perhaps it is a combination of the two. Some pupils develop such irrational fears without any overt form of bullying ever having taken place.

An obvious example is the case of absentees on their return to school. They walk back into their form room and hope to 'hide'. The moment the form tutor, or someone else, makes a pointed remark about their return to school, their anxieties are reinforced. It becomes harder for the pupil to return to school next time; easier to abscond or truant. No actual bullying has taken place, only insensitivity to the pupil's situation.

While most bullying of absentees is conducted by peers, frequently older pupils, this is not exclusively the case. Many absentees feel they are 'picked on', victimised by their teachers. Many teachers have very little time for their deviant pupils like absentees. They spend less constructive time on and with them. They get to know them less well. They use derogatory labels or terms to refer to them and expect the deviant behaviour to continue.

Pupils like absentees detect these messages. One of the tragedies of working with persistent absentees is that you come to realise so many of them are caught up in a truancy cycle. Some absentees will tell you: if only we could start again with a clean sheet. But they can't and they know it. Schooling is geared for conformists not deviants. In their fantasies they have good jobs, good incomes, happy home lives, are socially acceptable and good at everything. In reality, many of them are life's born losers and, as far as they are concerned, teachers don't help them. In fact, while absentees will make allowances for their parents, relatives and friends, they make no such allowances for their school or teachers (Reid, 1983b). They do not however, except in a few cases, blame their teacher for their plight. Rather, they tend to blame the school as an institution — the curriculum, rules and regulations, organisation, size, ethos and policies (Reid, 1983a,c). Only in the case of disruptive absentees is the reverse true (Reid, 1984a,b). In fact, except in the case of the disruptive absentee group, teacher-baiting and teacher bullying is not in their bag of tricks (Reid, 1988).

Jason: A Case Study

Jason is the third of three children. He lives on a council estate with his mother, stepfather and two sisters who have left school and are currently employed by a large store in the city centre. Jason is of below average ability but claims he enjoys school whenever he attends, which is rarely. He was a regular attender during his primary school days when his reports spoke of him 'trying hard despite reading and number difficulties'.

Shortly after his transfer to the local comprehensive, his discernible problems increased. First, he was put into a form without any of his previous classmates from his local primary school. This upset him.

Second, he stopped receiving individual remedial tuition in maths, reading and language, as he was considered slightly more able than those in the designated remedial group for his year.

Third, he indicated at interview that he started to feel 'lost' in the big school. He failed to make new friends quickly and started being regarded by his new classmates as a loner. At breaks and lunch-times, he sought out his old friends to play with from his former primary school.

Fourth, he started to believe that some of his teachers did not like him. 'They don't have time for people like me. They only like the good workers and the people who are good at other things like James (a useful footballer and athlete) and Russell (who swims for his local team and won the Under 15 Welsh Championships)'.

Fifth, probably for the reasons outlined above, he started to fall further and further behind with his school work. When one of his friends from his primary school started 'mitching', Jason started to join him on his fishing trips.

Sixth, Jason's health was not wonderful. He was asthmatic and was allergic to a large number of items. He had to take an inhaler three times daily which tended to draw attention to his deficiencies.

Up to the end of the second year, Jason's attendance was never less than 85-90% in any one term. In Year 3 however, there was a dramatic decline in his rate of attendance at school, The cause, according to him, was that he started to become victimised by the boys in his form. It started because they perceived him as being 'useless' at everything — games, work, socialising *et seq*. Moreover, as a loner, and as a boy with a puny frame, he was perceived as fair game by his much larger and stronger classmates. At first, they started blaming him whenever there was an interruption in a lesson. He was blamed for problems such as failing to put up his hand when the teacher asked a question, held responsible for the perceived escalation of litter in the classroom, making smells and throwing pellets during a lesson — charges he vigorously denied to the general amusement of all those around him.

The escalation of these problems began to prey on 'his mind and he started to dislike his school, his classmates and his teachers. After a three week absence, his first of more than three consecutive days, he found his return to school a traumatic experience. First, he felt humiliated by his form tutor's comments about his mother's letter which according to the teacher was fictional, badly expressed and full of spelling mistakes. The tutor suggested that it was obvious from where Jason's educational limitations accrued. Second, his classmates had carved comments about his inabilities all over his desk during his absence. Third, the detrimental comments changed to acts of bullying and victimisation at breaks and lunch-times. In the beginning it was 'names' being called out followed by jocular bouts of pinching his bottom and hiding his coat and shoes. Later, after Jason had cried one morning, the bullying increased in intensity and started to include more malicious acts. Immediately, Jason started staying away from school for long periods of continued absence, only returning for short spells after home visits from the education welfare officer. By the end of the fourth year, he had been taken to court for truancy and his school report spoke of 'no progress whatsoever as he is never present'.

Analysis of Jason's data showed that he had a low academic self-concept, a low level of general self-esteem, felt alienated from school, was of below average intelligence, had fewer friends than most of his peers, showed signs of neuroticism while he generally felt unhappy about attending school.

In his interviews he stated that he would return to school and attend regularly if:

1) they stopped the bullying and changed his form;
2) they provided him with regular remedial tuition in reading and maths (he was chronically aware of his deficiencies in the basic subjects);
3) the teachers stopped making adverse comments about his lack of ability in lessons.

According to the education welfare officer, Jason missed school because of his poor home background and intellectual abilities. His form teacher claimed hardly to know him but singled out his unfavourable home background for his non-attendance. His head of year believed his absence was due to his mother's influence. At no stage did the school acknowledge any institutional dimension to Jason's problems such as bullying and general unhappiness with his form group.

Conclusions

Summarising, my research suggests that bullying is a significant factor in the genesis and escalation of school absenteeism in a minority of cases. The absentees as victims tend to be vulnerable, to have low self-concepts, to be defenceless, to exaggerate or worry about perceived or actual threats, to draw attention to themselves through their behaviour, temperament or personality and, in a clear minority of cases, to invite retribution through their own aggressive stances.

Although research has still to confirm this possibility, I believe the incidence of bullying and bullying related to absenteeism will vary from school to school. Key factors will include school size, school ethos, teacher-pupil relationships, peer group relationships, the quality of pastoral care, school policies on special educational needs and remedial education and, finally, and crucially, school policies on bullying. When schools have no policies on acts of bullying or do not recognise its existence, the situation is normally made worse.

My research clearly demonstrated that school staff were unaware that a significant proportion of their absentees stayed away from school because they had been or were afraid of coming to school, being in school and/or of returning to school. They were also oblivious to the pupil extortion endemic in one school. If school staff are unaware of the causes of absenteeism from their own institutions, and sometimes hardly care, then defenceless and vulnerable pupils like absentees such as Jason are forced to look after themselves. Given their lack of social, physical or intellectual strength, it is easier to opt out, to run away from the threat.

References

Reid, K. (1982). The self-concept and persistent school absenteeism, *British Journal of Educational Psychology,* 52, 2, 179-87.

Reid, K. (1983a). Retrospection and persistent school absenteeism, *Educational Research,* 2, 25, 110-115.

Reid, K. (1983b). Differences between the perception of persistent absentees towards parents and teachers, *Educational Studies,* 9, 3, 211-19.

Reid, K. (1983c). Institutional factors and persistent school absenteeism, *Journal of Educational Management and Administration,* 11, 17-27.

Reid, K. (1984a). The behaviour of persistent school absentees, *British Journal of Educational Psychology,* 54, 320-330.

Reid, K. (1984b). Disruptive behaviour and persistent school absenteeism. In Frude, N. and Gault, H. (eds.) *Disruptive Behaviour in Schools.* John Wiley.

Reid, K. (1985). *Truancy and School Absenteeism.* Hodder and Stoughton.

Reid, K. (1986a). *Disaffection From School.* Methuen.

Reid, K. (1986b). Truancy and school absenteeism: The state of the art, *Maladjustment and Therapeutic Education,* 4, 3, 4-17.

Reid, K. (1987a). *Combating School Absenteeism.* Hodder and Stoughton.

Reid, K. (1987b). See chapters 1, 2, 6, 9, 12, 15, 19 and 21 in *Combating School Absenteeism.* Hodder and Stoughton.

Reid, K. (1988). Bullying, chapter in Reid, K. (ed.) *Helping Troubled Pupils in Secondary Schools,* Volume 2. Blackwell.

Chapter 9
Violent Histories: Bullying and Criminality
David A. Lane

Just walking through the school you can feel the undercurrent of violence, to continue to send my son to the school is unthinkable.

> (parent visiting son's school)

This is a boy's school. You have to accept bullying. If a child can't take it they should be in another school.

> (teacher at the same school)

This parent and teacher agree: the child should be in another school. But is bullying so inevitable and is moving the victim the only solution? This chapter suggests otherwise. It is argued that bullying is a complex process, of which the philosophy and practice of the school is a part. Schools can act and by doing so they not only prevent untold suffering for the victim but also reduce the incidence of later violent criminality. As a number of studies show, (Robbins, 1966; West and Farrington, 1973; Lane, 1983) problems in childhood are reflected in the adult criminal statistics.

The Islington Educational Guidance Centre Research Series
The Islington EGC provides support services to schools, parents and pupils in areas related to behaviour difficulties. Its approach to provision has always been informed by a research orientation (Lane, 1974, 1978, 1986). Over a period of 15 years the research series at the Islington Centre has traced the lives of its pupils. This work formed part of a study under the auspices of a research trust, The Professional Development Foundation, which includes a data base extending over 20 years and around three thousand children and several hundred parents and teachers.

In fairness to Islington schools, it must be pointed out that the research data have been collected in a number of areas, including both Conservative and Labour held LEA's. Islington schools are no more problematic than schools in many other parts of the country.

The research considered certain basic questions:

1. What is bullying?
2. What factors are relevant to an understanding of bullying?
3. What can be done to prevent bullying?
4. What are the long term outcomes of the bullying experience?

1. What is bullying?
Bullying is one of those difficult concepts: everyone can define it but when you seek examples it can lead to confusion. Most people would include in their

definition some sense of threat, but must it also include violence? It probably includes a sense of fear but must the bully have intended that fear or is causing fear sufficient without direct intent? (We were just larking about!) Is causing fear on one occasion bullying or must it be repeated to count?

The definition used in this study is similar to the legal term 'Threatening Behaviour'. Bullying is therefore taken to include any action or implied action, such as threats or violence, intended to cause fear and distress. Unlike the legal definition, the behaviour had to be repeated on more than one occasion. The definition includes the concept of intention and therefore cannot be based simply on the observation of a teacher, but must include evidence that those involved intended or felt fear. School records referring to acts of bullying or extortion were, consequently, supplemented with interviews to establish intent. Since the data itself is likely to under-report and individuals had to admit to their acts, the amount of identified bullying is probably an underestimate.

Bullying may take a variety of forms from the obvious to the more subtle, for example:

a) A group of three fourth year secondary boys demanding money from first years.

b) A ten year old who controlled the behaviour of others in the playground by hitting anyone who disagreed, and systematically attacked one girl who tried to stand up to him.

c) A 15 year old boy who was fearful of another group of boys. They would play threatening games on him to see how scared he would get.

d) A group of fourth year girls who controlled access to the toilets at break times. A girl they did not like was systematically excluded, so that she could neither urinate nor change a sanitary towel.

e) A fifth year girl who intensely disliked a Muslim girl in her class, and organised her friends to ignore her. For added fun she then pretended to be friends, persuaded the girl to organise a party at her house, and then ensured that no one came.

f) An English teacher who would control difficult pupils by systematically humiliating them, by asking those who had severe reading difficulties to read out loud in class and then encouraging others to comment negatively.

g) A Maths teacher who, knowing which pupils were beaten at home, would threaten to send letters home about discipline problems in the classroom.

Some of the above would not count as bullying but the distress experienced was real. To be identified as an act of bullying it had to be intended but also it had to be experienced (labelled) as such. In most practical rather than research contexts the labeller is someone in a position of power, therefore the child is a bully, a teacher is not.

Using the definition of bullying above, a study was undertaken to look at the extent of bullying and its duration. As part of a broader study which included, for example, information on background factors, personality, and school progress, four sets of data were collected.

Sample 1: This looked at a random group of 100 pupils from a mixed secondary school. Pupils were individually interviewed. A feature of these interviews was the number of incidents reported which to the outside observer would have seemed like bullying but which the pupils did not define as such. Approximately a fifth (19%) of the pupils defined themselves as being involved in bullying as victim, perpetrator or both. They also identified about 10% of staff members as bullies. The most disturbing aspect of the data was the duration of the problem: most identified their difficulties as victims as extending over at least a year, and often 2 to 3 years.

Sample 2: This looked at 60 pupils from the same school who were noted as having behaviour problems. Of this group some 43% identified themselves as being involved in bullying. Of those who were primarily victims, the duration often exceeded two years.

Sample 3: This looked at a random group of 120 pupils in a girls' secondary school. The results were broadly similar to sample 1, in terms of level but not type of incidents. Girls were reporting 'psychological' and physical threats as bullying, whereas boys tended to see bullying in physical terms.

Sample 4: This looked at 200 pupils across the age range, referred for behaviour problems from a number of different schools. Of this group some 57% were involved.

That figure seemed high and in a subsequent sample obtained as part of a separate study, a figure of 38% was obtained. One feature distinguishing the first sample was the larger number of pupils involved in delinquency in the first group. These samples gave rise to the idea of looking at the link between bullying and later 'violent histories'.

It is difficult to determine the level of bullying that is likely to exist but it is apparent from Stephenson and Smith's (1987) work with a much larger sample that these levels are in line with their data.

2. What factors are relevant to an understanding of bullying?

The research programme has concentrated on long term studies of children who fail to respond to traditional interventions for problem behaviour, the 'Impossible Child'. (Lane, 1978). A large number of these pupils include Bullying as part of the problem profile and studies have therefore been undertaken looking at them, the victim and features of school response which increase difficulties. Four explanations for the continuation of problems were explored, and a brief summary of those explanations is helpful to place the behaviour in context. (Full data is reported in Lane, 1983).

Personality: It has been argued that behaviour difficulties are more likely in individuals who report themselves to be toughminded, stable extraverts. A series of studies investigating this explanation have been undertaken. The results show a complex relationship between characteristics of the individual and their situation, but do point to predictive effects on such areas as levels of problem behaviour, response to discipline and therapy, and long term delinquency.

97

Individual differences in pattern of response are of equal importance in relation to bullying and victim reaction. Bullying is an example of acute stress and the way an individual develops 'coping skills' to deal with such stress situations has important implications for later response to areas such as unemployment and serious illness (Lane, 1989). Understanding a child's personal style of response is therefore an important part of the development of effective preventive strategies.

Multiple stress: The idea that those who present difficulties in school are likely to have multiple disadvantages has long been argued (Lane, 1978; Wall, 1979). In this study, a number of candidates for a role in multiple stress were investigated. A consistent pattern was found. Those most likely to have difficulties were found to have:

a)   more health problems,
b)   lower social class membership,
c)   poor peer relationships,
d)   larger families,
e)   higher levels of disadvantage in their families,
f)   lower levels of compensating positive features in their families.

Those involved in bullying were also more likely to be seen by teachers as 'bad children' not just badly behaved. This result was found even on data obtained prior to any record of bullying. Bullies and victims, and those who fell into both categories, were often seen as 'physically unattractive' people by teachers.

Those most likely to improve following periods of difficulty showed the opposite characteristics. The absence of positive compensating features was found to be as important as the presence of the negative.

Behaviour predicts itself: It has been demonstrated in a number of studies that behaviour problems in school predict future difficulties. This idea was tested in a series of follow up studies using five year periods. The results supported the prediction. Sadly, how a child was viewed in infant school did correlate with the rating obtained ten years later. However, the consistency of reports during school career was not as great as that result suggested. In some schools, with some teachers, even those with major problems worked well and behaved appropriately. This was particularly marked in a study of 100 pupils who were presenting difficulties over several years. An attempt to look at the underlying pattern in the complex maze of contributing features, (using a technique known as factor analysis) did indicate that beyond the behaviour itself, the most important feature concerned the events that subsequently happened to the child. The continuation of family deprivation or its alleviation was important but so, crucially, was the action taken by the child's school. *Schools did make a difference.*

Behaviour problems left untreated do improve: This concept, spontaneous remission, is well established. It was tested in the study using follow up samples and found to hold true for some difficulties more than others. However, it was also true that intervention prolonged the problems for some children. The labelling of children as difficult was found to operate as a self-fulfilling prophecy. The importance of recognising that behaviour is defined by reference to an individual, a social context, and someone in a position of power, was paramount. The same behaviour was labelled very differently both within and between classes in the same school, and across schools. Children exhibiting similar levels of difficulty in a given school, some of whom were labelled and some not, were found to be subsequently rated by their teachers as more difficult in the absence of objective evidence for the claim. Once a child was labelled, it was very difficult for him or her to 'prove they were a reformed character'. The beliefs within a school about the nature of behaviour problems and the structures used to deal with them were part of the problem as well as sometimes being part of the solution.

The problem is complex. There is no simple answer. But solutions exist.

For example: a violent history with a happy ending?

John was the youngest of five children. His father was in regular work but, according to the mother's and child's account, had always been aggressive towards the children. At one time she would intervene to prevent the children being hit, but after receiving beatings herself, gave up the attempt. She reported that he had a poor relationship with all the children. A number of attempts over the years to involve the family in Family Therapy failed. The older brother had been suspended from school for bullying and was increasingly involved with the police. John spent several months in hospital in his early years needing a series of operations to correct birth defects. He remembered that period clearly, feeling very frightened. Difficulties with language development added to his problems. Speech therapy over several years and two years in a specialist unit for language difficulties and later a period in a unit for the 'emotionally disturbed', preceeded his transfer to mainstream secondary education. At this time he was still a nonreader and had poorly developed social skills, although his speech had improved. He developed a severe stutter at the age of twelve. At this time he increasingly became involved in violence and vandalism and, subsequently, football hooliganism.

The school he attended made extensive use of the cane as a punishment, in spite of the fact that, as the Deputy Head said, 'You might as well cane the wall as some of these children for all the good it does'. (Such non-response to discipline and therapy was a feature of many of the toughminded, stable extravert children in the study).

In terms of the research findings reported above, we have an example of a child with multiple problems. However, there were also several positive compensatory features. He had established a very good relationship with the special needs teacher in the school, who made a determined and successful attempt to teach him to read. A number of other teachers felt there were positive aspects in his behaviour although they neither accepted nor tolerated his bullying. Several teachers wanted him further beaten, suspended, prosecuted or 'xxxxed'. His mother, although unable to act against the father, did provide a compassionate model and he felt loved by her.

The school decided to make a referral for Child Guidance but that broke down. (Psychotherapy is often sought, 'perhaps he needs individual help', but rarely useful for a toughminded, extravert pupil, who has learned a pattern of violent response and has been consistently reinforced for using it). They then made a referral to the Islington Centre. A complex analysis and intervention followed. In brief, it identified certain key elements:

a) Both his father and some male teachers provided models of aggressive behaviour. John disliked them but saw them as powerful models.

b) He valued the compassion he was shown but saw that as weakness.

c) He greatly valued being in school, at least that part of it which gave him some sense of success. He feared the prospect of further suspension.

d) His speech difficulty and lack of social skills prevented his expressing/asserting himself effectively. When confronted, he found that hitting out worked: children did not tease you if you terrorised them, and being unpredictable made teachers uncertain about confronting you. Violence worked, reason did not.

e) The school did not have a consistent policy, and conflicts between staff were apparent in dealing with these issues and this pupil.

A programme was introduced to teach him mechanisms to deal with stress situations and to develop his social skills. A review of the models in his environment took place, to help him to identify power as legitimate assertion rather than aggression. A contracted set of relationships were established with teachers so that events became predictable with defined *consequences*. It was made clear that any incident of bullying would be followed by a suspension, but that the issue of provocation by others would also be tackled, that is, he saw it as fair. Over a nine month period the programme took effect with only two incidents being reported. No violence was reported in his final year at school. He left without qualifications but did eventually obtain work. Two years later he was involved in an incident with others (his old football gang) but, following a period of probation and good social work support, stayed out of further trouble. Five years on he was working, developing an ongoing relationship and feeling positive about himself.

Underlying themes

Although this case history represents a simplified account of the work, it does raise the issue of the interrelationship of individual, family, and school elements. There were also underlying themes in this school which were important features, and were reflected in other schools in the research study.

Power and masculinity . . . an ambivalence of attitudes to such issues in a school influences the behaviour that occurs. Bullying as a status activity and the attitude taken towards the bully is a part of the reinforcement available for bullying.

Reinforcement and control . . . the school staff reflected inconsistent attitudes to the need to reinforce the idea that children are entitled to feel valued and safe, as opposed to the idea that you control bad behaviour by punishment.

A failure to deal with these issues clouds attempts by a school to state a clear policy on issues involving respect for others. A policy on equal opportunities for race, sex and class is ineffective if, for example, women teachers working in a boys' school feel intimated by the tactics of male staff towards them (an issue raised by staff at this school). If a school does not create an atmosphere in which children feel valued and safe, they are less likely to report not only bullying but also abuse that takes place outside of school. There may be a number of stereotypes operating which are unhelpful. The bully as a lout or the victim as a wimp, are popular concepts, but are misleading. Victims may be weak, tough, themselves bully, provoke acts or be the passive recipient; girls as well as boys are involved, and pupils may also operate a variety of sexual stereotypes to explain the behaviour. Understanding the beliefs that operate in a particular school is important if a whole school policy is to be effective (Lane, 1989). Schools with similar catchment areas do vary greatly in the level of bullying which takes place and even within classes in the same school the level of aggressive as opposed to cooperative behaviour which occurs is a consistent factor.

3. What can be done to prevent bullying?

Most important by far is for the school itself to have a policy on which it acts. A whole school approach is a prerequisite for effective action (see Herbert Ch. 6).

A whole school policy is most likely to be possible when the members of the community of the school have thought through their attitudes on equal opportunities, and believe sufficiently in that policy to create an environment in which staff, parents and pupils feel valued and safe (see Askew, Ch. 5 and Titman, Ch. 10).

Given the above, to the extent that it is true that multiple disadvantage is a factor, the relationship between a school and the support services in the community is vital (Reid, Ch. 8; Lane and Tattum, 1989). Too often, mutual hostility exists in this area. If social services do not trust the school, and vice versa, how can help be offered to 'John' or his mother?

The fact that bullying is a complex pattern, which affects all schools and ages, must be recognised (Chazan, Ch. 3; Walford, Ch. 7 and Stephenson and Smith, Ch. 4). One solution is unlikely to be helpful for all situations. Victims are empowered if they feel safe to report and have been taught the skills to respond to threatening situations (Roland Ch. 2).

These issues represent areas for whole school response but beyond these key points lies the area of specific action in relation to particular victims, bullies, and bully/victims. As the case study of John indicated, the action taken must depend on a clear analysis of the factors which influence the particular situation. An automatic appeal to punishment or therapy is destructive. Therapy can work, punishment can work, both can if inappropriately applied increase the complexity of the situation. An individual assessment based on a systematic model of analysis can (must) be applied to behaviour labelled as bullying. If you understand the interrelationship between individual, family and school factors, a realistic intervention can be planned that will be effective (Lane, 1978).

In making a case for individual analysis, we have sometimes been accused of being 'soft' on bullies. It is, therefore, important to stress that individual analysis follows the establishment of a school policy, which clearly encourages the sense of value and safety of pupils and staff alike. When 'criminal assaults' took place, our own practice was to encourage parents of victims or staff to make a complaint to the Police. We felt that individuals should face the consequences of their actions. However, once that action had been taken, we would make a variety of recommendations to the Juvenile Bureau, based on an analysis of the specific case (Lane, 1985).

What are the long term effects of the bullying experience?

It was argued above that behaviour in school does predict later criminality, and Tattum (Ch. 1) has demonstrated the relationship between disruption and later patterns of crime. This relationship has also been discussed elsewhere (Lane and Hymans, 1981; Topping, 1983; Lane, 1987). Two important features will, however, be considered.

Delinquent careers: A sample of 250 pupils was followed. The pattern of delinquency over a five year period, extending to ten in the case of those who became delinquent, was examined. Subsequent delinquency was found to be predictable from previously obtained personality data (Lane, 1987). In addition (Lane, 1983) data was obtained on a group of 100 pupils who presented problems over a period of time. A continuity of behaviour ratings from teachers from infant to the final years of secondary schooling was obtained. The pupils were seen not only as badly behaved but as bad people who were similarly at loggerheads with adults and peers. Their subsequent delinquent careers extended their conflict with others from a period, in some cases, stretching from five to twenty years of age. This raises important questions as to the sources of support available to such pupils lacking in social contacts and reinforcement.

It was a feature of the data that generally boys were more likely to develop delinquent careers than girls. However, those girls who became involved in bullying and delinquency tended to be more delinquent than a comparative group of boys. In a sample of 30 followed over five years the girls averaged 4.4 convictions compared with 2.2 for the boys. Some of the groups studied proved to be particularly delinquent. A group of 20 pupils labelled as 'impossible' by their teachers were subsequently found to average 15.9 convictions, and 14 of these pupils had convictions for violence.

These patterns did indicate a relationship between bullying and violent crime (see also Tattum, Ch. 1). The complexity of this for the individual child was notable, e.g. individuals trying to get out of patterns of crime found their records following them. For some, in the absence of an employer, starting their own business proved to be the only avenue open, mostly in the alternative economy (Lane, 1989). Individuals with a string of convictions for assault and robbery, ranted about the 'scum who would mug old ladies'. The variety of beliefs, rationalisations, and personal histories of pain really did generate confusion in professional action. At what point does the physically and sexually abused child, who hits out at others, and therefore is in 'need of therapy', become the violent thug in 'need of the birch'? Children with an obvious handicap elicit sympathy, but if their pain is expressed in a sullen violence they elicit revenge.

Intervention patterns: In tracing the pattern of delinquent behaviour, the traditional graph of a rise from around 13/14 years of age appeared. It was found, however, that effective intervention by the school (and some agencies) to create alternatives to the escalation in delinquency which takes place in the final years of secondary schooling, did have long term effects. Delinquency could, in a significant number of cases (although not all), be prevented (Topping, 1983; Lane, 1987):

For example, a group of 120 pupils (successful and unsuccessful therapy groups and a non-disruptive control) were considered in terms of subsequent delinquency and it was found that the successful group, while more delinquent than the control, were significantly less delinquent that the unsuccessful group.

The pattern of delinquency for these pupils over the age range 10 to 21 years revealed increased delinquency for all three groups between the ages of 14 to 17 and a decrease from 18 to 21 years. The two therapy groups were not significantly different prior to the therapeutic interventions but became so with time. The key period seemed to be the ages 14 to 17. Effective action in that period slowed down the level of criminal activity. A review of the histories of the pupils studied did show that where preventive action was not taken, a spiral into persistent delinquency was more likely. In too many cases the child later became the adult convicted of assault, grievous bodily harm, indecent assault, and so on up through an escalating catalogue of violent crime. Victims who were helped fared better. Those who were not, fared less well. Some learnt that violence paid, some found themselves needing subsequent psychiatric help. Saddest of all were those worked with as bullied and abused children, who then as parents became the abusers of their own children (Lane, 1989).

In conclusion

Violent incidents and ongoing intimidation in schools is more likely when the school itself fails to take the issue seriously. If a senior member of staff concurs with the view that:

This is a boys' school. You have to accept bullying. If a child can't take it, they should be in another school,

then bullying is likely to flourish. Similarly, if the school felt unable to act in case it 'made the situation worse', then the situation became worse.

It has proved possible in this, (Lane, 1975; Lane and Tattum 1989) and other studies reported in this volume, to teach children to feel safe and to deal with bullying:

a)   through a specific social skills programme;
b)   through action to support the child bullied;
c)   through action to work with the bully;
d)   through action by the school to change its own practice.

It has proved possible to teach children to feel valued and not to bully.

a)   through assessment of the factors giving rise to the behaviour;
b)   through planned action;
c)   through action to demonstrate support for the victim;
d)   through action by the school to change its own practice.

Effective action is possible and change can be maintained.

The alternative to approaching the problem on the basis of evidence and a pragmatic, rather than a politicised, attitude to intervention is not a matter of conjecture, as the long term studies show.

These children cannot be hidden and will not go away, but will as adults, reap with destruction what we sow now with neglect.

References

Lane, D.A. (1974) The behavioural analysis of complex cases. Conference Paper IEGC, London.

Lane, D.A. (1975) *Dependency: techniques of prevention*. IEGC/Kings Fund, London.

Lane, D.A. (1978) *The Impossible Child Vol. 1 & 2*. Inner London Education Authority.

Lane, D.A. (1983) *Whatever happened to the Impossible Child?* Inner London Education Authority.

Lane, D.A. (1985) The use of psychological reports in the Juvenile Court. In Gudjonsson, G. and Drinkwater, J. (1987) *Psychological Evidence in Court*. British Psychological Society, Leicester.

Lane, D.A. (1986) Promoting positive behaviour in the classroom. In Tattum, D.P. (Ed.) (1986) *Management of Disruptive Pupil Behaviour in Schools*. John Wiley.

Lane, D.A. (1987) Personality and antisocial behaviour a long term study. *Personality and Individual Differences*. Vol. 8.6, pp.799-806.

Lane, D.A. (1989) *The Impossible Child or the Lost Entrepreneur*. Professional Development Foundation/Trentham Books.

Lane, D.A., and Hymans, M.H. (1982) The prediction of delinquency. *Personality and Individual Differences*. Vol. 3, pp.87-88.

Lane, D.A., and Tattum, D.P. (1989) *Supporting the child in school*. Open University Press.

Robbins, L.N. (1966) *Deviant Children Grown Up*. Williams & Williams, Baltimore.

Stephenson, P., and Smith, D. (1987) Anatomy of a playground bully. *Education* 18.9, 1987.

Topping, K. (1983) *Educational Systems For Disruptive Adolescents*. Croom Helm.

Wall, W.D. (1979) *Constructive Education for Special Groups*. Harrap.

West, D., and Farrington, D.P. (1973) *Who Becomes Delinquent?* Heinemann.

Chapter 10
Adult Responses to Children's Fears: Including Resource Materials
Wendy Titman

Adult images of childhood and play

Childhood is a neglected subject. We cannot condone a lack of understanding or prejudice towards the things we have never experienced, though it is possible to understand how such reactions ensue from ignorance. However, to all who live long enough to reach adulthood, childhood, like death, is one of the few certainties of living. The quality of the experience will vary but there is no escaping the fact that every adult has been through a period which we have come to call childhood. Yet for many, if not most adults, it is a time of their lives which is forgotten, they 'grew up' and in the process either lost or distorted the memories, thoughts, feelings and reactions of a large portion of their life.

Images of childhood are currently very fashionable. On greetings cards, prints and pictures, healthy, happy children in Victorian dress are seen playing in green fields or by the sea. Sadly these are the remnants of the propaganda of that era, created to counteract the reality of the plight of the majority of Britain's children in the nineteenth century.

The propaganda of childhood lives on. It is assumed and expected that everyone enjoyed their childhood. As the subject is rarely discussed amongst adults, the assumption is relatively safe. There is a vague feeling that any qualification of one's personal experience would amount to an admission of failure. When pressed, few would claim that their childhood constituted a state of total happiness and unencumbered joy. Being a child brings confusion, fear, anxiety, uncertainty and considerable stress. It is a learning process and for all who live a relatively 'normal' life, these feelings are inevitable. Perhaps this explains why most adults have little accurate recall of their childhood years — growing up provides its own defence mechanism against painful memories. Whatever the reason, the fact that few adults are conscious of their childhood, creates considerable problems for each new generation of children.

There are a variety of aspects of childhood about which we understand very little. Until relatively recently the phenomenon of play has been either widely misunderstood or totally ignored. The fact that we learn through play is a glib and often quoted statement. However, there has been relatively little research into the subject and there remains widely differing views of how it should be accommodated and provided for — if at all.

More often than not, when the subject of bullying is raised it is in the context of school and, more particularly, in terms of the school playground. The nineteenth century concept that children needed a break between lessons in which to 'run around and get some fresh air' was consistent with the understanding of the role of education at that time. Classrooms may have altered; the process by which we educate children certainly has, but it is still all too common to find that the school playground remains the barren area it was in Victorian times.

For the modern day child, stimulated by all that education can offer, the playground can be a boring, hostile and barren place. An open expanse of tarmac, bordered by buildings, walls and fences providing nothing with which a child may interact, explore or experiment, is a breeding ground for bullying. Where such problems are perceived, it is often assumed that greater supervision is necessary, presumably in order to suppress such behaviour or to enable a greater degree of intervention and arbitration. One school recently introduced the concept of red and yellow cards, an idea borrowed from the football field, as a means of regulating playground behaviour. Often it seems we are drawn to finding curative rather than preventative strategies for dealing with childhood issues and problems.

A lack of knowledge of the importance of children's play and particularly the behaviour of children at play, is a substantial barrier to dealing with behavioural problems in the playground. More importantly, this lack of understanding minimises the potential for creating an atmosphere which utilises the school play area as a positive extension of the learning environment created inside school.

In a two year study based at a first and middle school in Oxford, Sluckin (1981) studied the social world of children during playtime through noting what the children did and said to each other. In his book *Growing up in the Playground* he concludes:

> I hoped that observing the playground world would lead teachers to share my conclusions. First, that children are learning all sorts of social skills and second, that in activities of their own choice children are much more sophisticated than could be guessed from their classroom performance.

Of course children will and do play anywhere, wherever they are and without being organised. Equally, they will argue, quarrel and even fight during play, whether at home with siblings, in the street with friends, in the school playground or in other types of organised play environments. A degree of conflict during play is inevitable and provides a valuable way for children to learn that people are different, and for them to develop skills to understand conflict and find ways of dealing with differences and conflict.

Iona and Peter Opie devoted their lifetime's work to the study of traditional children's games. Their published works provide a fascinating insight into the ways in which, over many centuries, children developed songs, rhymes, chants and customs as a means of dealing with potential conflict situations during their play. This is particularly evident in the use of rhymes rather than personal choice as a means of selecting who is 'in' and who is 'out' when playing certain games (Opie and Opie, 1959; 1969).

It is arguable whether traditional games still feature prominently in children's lives and whether, for today's children, such strategies can provide 'child-centred' solutions to problems such as bullying, without some form of adult intervention.

The prevalence of reports of bullying and aggression in school playgrounds raises an interesting question about children's play behaviour in other supervised settings.

Where play is supervised, the behaviour of children is undoubtedly affected by three main elements: firstly, by the presence of adults and the nature of supervision, secondly, by the degree of freedom of participation and, thirdly, by the environment in which playing takes place.

There are many reasons why children require and may benefit from being supervised whilst at play, not only during school playtime but also during their 'out of school' time. The past two decades has seen a growth in the provision of supervised playcentres, playgrounds and after school clubs for young children, though provision is still inadequate across the country as a whole. The nature of such facilities and the services they offer will vary but the common element of supervision has led to the creation of playwork as a career — some would say a profession.

The role of the playworker is complex and multi-faceted. Essentially it relies upon the ability to facilitate, encourage and enable children to gain maximum benefit from their 'play time'. It requires the ability to interact with individual children whilst relating to large numbers, of different ages, often at the same time! Inevitably the ability to control such situations is vital, but, ideally, should never be obvious in the normal course of events. A good playworker relies heavily upon a relationship of mutual trust and respect with children and has few if any authoritarian sanctions available if the relationship breaks down. Involvement with children during their play can pre-empt and prevent problems arising and is thus a preferred management style to supervising them.

If relationships between children and playworkers do for any reason break down, or if control of children's behaviour is inadequate, enabling bullying and victimisation to take place, some children will exercise freedom of choice and not use the facility. Such facilities rely upon demand and those which fail to attract children, for whatever reason, are unlikely to continue operating. As a result, all kinds of strategies are employed by playworkers to prevent behavioural problems occurring and much valuable expertise has been developed for working successfully with children in such settings. Sadly, there is still no single nationally recognised qualification for playworkers, though a great deal of excellent training is provided at local and regional level. A new national organisation, The Children's Play Unit, was set up in 1988 to promote standards in play and playwork and will, once established, be able to give information about playwork training opportunities.[1]

The third element of importance in the provision of supervised play for children is that of the environment in which it takes place. In his book, *Children's domain — play and place in child development,* Moore (1986) presents unique research which demonstrates the significance of the environment on children's play and its effect on their development and behaviour. Whilst this work concentrated fundamentally on the environments in which children play outside school, it presents some important information about the correlation between the management of environments and the management of children in them.

Schools that set about improving the playground environment often find a commesurate improvement in the behaviour and attitudes of children using it. To anyone who can remember playtime, this is not surprising. Efforts to improve playgrounds by totally changing the landscape and design can be expensive. Many schools have made significant improvements to their playgrounds by the creation of gardens and 'quiet areas', or by organising mural schemes incorporating games and puzzles on tarmac and wall spaces — all of which cost only time and effort.

A new, three-year research project called 'Learning through Landscapes'[2] established in 1986, aims to investigate the potential of school grounds as a resource for learning and teaching; to investigate design and management practices and to report on the design, management and use of school grounds in relation to improving environmental quality and educational opportunity. Whilst essentially concerned with environmental issues, the project is also dealing with the social and behavioural aspects of the use of school playgrounds by children. The project published details of the first phase of its work — 'The Design, Management and Use of School Grounds, Setting the Perameters' in 1988. This document will be of interest to any school considering the issue of management of play space and its effect on children's behaviour.

This section on the relationship between the play environment and children's behaviour ends with an eloquent perspective on life in a school playground:

Back in the Playground Blues

Dreamed I was in a school playground, I was about four feet high
Yes dreamed I was back in the playground, and standing about four feet high
The playground was three miles long and the playground was five miles wide

It was broken black tarmac with a high fence all around
Broken black dusty tarmac with a high fence running all around
And it had a special name to it, they called it The Killing Ground.

Got a mother and a father, they're a thousand miles away
The Rulers of the Killing Ground are coming out to play
Everyone thinking: who they going to play with today?

    You get it for being Jewish
    Get it for being black
    Get it for being chicken
    Get it for fighting back

You get it for being big and fat
Get it for being small
O those who get it get it and get it
For any damn thing at all
Sometimes they take a beetle, tear off its six legs one by one
Beetle on its black back rocking in the lunchtime sun
But a beetle can't beg for mercy, a beetle's not half the fun

Heard a deep voice talking, it had that iceberg sound;
'It prepares them for Life' — but I have never found
Any place in my life that's worse than The Killing Ground.

ADRIAN MITCHELL (Rosen, 1985)

Adult ambivalence towards aggressive behaviour

In terms of bullying, adult reactions and responses vary from — 'It's just part of growing up', and, 'You have to learn to stand up for yourself', to the classic, 'Sticks and stones can break your bones but words can never hurt you'. Only an adult could have created that piece of rhyming nonsense!

When aspects associated with childhood encroach into the adult world the reaction is very different. A remarkable example of this was the national outcry in response to publicity about bullying in the armed forces. Such was the disgust of the public at large that debates took place in the House and politicians called for a special inquiry. Yet the little research into bullying shows that a relatively high percentage of children are affected by incidents of bullying on a regular and on-going basis.

Rarely do adults admit to having suffered as children from bullying. Sir Rannulph Fiennes, the explorer, recounted in an interview his misery in childhood because of persistent bullying at school. As his physical appearance seemed to be the cause of the victimisation, he took up boxing. Not long afterwards, in a tribute to the TV personality Eamonn Andrews, it was explained that his career as a boxing commentator grew from his having been a keen amateur boxer. He was apparently introduced to the sport by his father because he was being bullied at school.

If violence amongst and between children is common, it is inevitable that this behaviour will spill over from the playground and become apparent in the 'real world'. Research indicates that children who manifest severe conduct disorders or anti-social behaviour are likely to display problems of adjustment in adolescence and adulthood (Lane, Ch. 9). Furthermore, without considerable — and appropriate — help, they will not 'grow out of it' and, in learning to cope, may create major problems for themselves and everyone around them. Society recognises the problem of violent and anti-social behaviour amongst young people at the stage when adult society displays scant regard for its laws. As the ability to commit certain crimes is, in law, age related, recognition of the problem is also age related. It is now quite common to hear politicians and others proclaim a deep concern about the growth of incidents of violence involving young people. Yet, despite an awareness of, and attention to the issues in the broadest sense, there is little agreement as to the fundamental causes of this trend. Interest therefore is directed towards curative and retributive measures rather than to more constructive, preventative approaches.

We know that children learn through experience and example. The degree to which children are exposed to violence is recognised as being a contributing factor to their behaviour patterns, yet many adults would deny the effect of violence on television on children's attitudes and behaviour. This is all the more remarkable when one looks at the advertising budgets of companies which use television as a marketing medium. Judging from the vast sums involved, advertising a product on television must influence people to purchase it. A recent study in America revealed that by age thirteen, some children will have witnessed 10,000 'deaths' on television and videos.

The controversy also continues about the involvement of children in competitive sport. The processes of selection for participation in games, which children have devised over generations, are complex and, to the adult, often quite bizarre. The ritualistic songs, rhymes and actions which provide the means of 'joining in' or 'being out' are still sacrosanct. Fascinating in themselves, these rituals demonstrate clearly that children have an innate sense of justice and injustice and will often resort to luck rather than any meaningful process of selection. Sport and game playing literally, has been adulterated. If children today display an overtly aggressive 'win at all cost' attitude, we should look to adult example for the cause. Sadly, many sporting personalities are either oblivious of, or careless about, the effects of their actions and attitudes on children.

Adults as models

For many children, everyday experiences may lead them to feel that rude and aggressive behaviour is not only the way to succeed but quite normal. A recent research study (Yule, 1985) observed parents and children in the street. Pairs of adults were compared with pairs consisting of an adult and a small child. Within a three minute observation period of each pair, four-fifths of the adult pairs had some speech with each other, or communicated with a glance or a smile. By contrast, less than half of the adult/child pairs had any positive communication. The report went on to detail that children were smacked, scolded, dragged across roads, while the children themselves cried, tried to talk to the adults and were persistently ignored. Yule wonders at the widespread rudeness of adults to children. 'What has happened to make parents now feel incompetent, martyred and irritable? Why can't they enjoy their children?' She concludes that it is part of a total social problem which gives young mothers feelings of low status and incompetence. For the purposes of this chapter we may speculate further about the relevance of the findings for learned aggressive behaviour and children's perceptions of adults.

There are obviously all kinds of reasons why leaving children to learn about relationships totally by example might not be appropriate or desirable. Whilst adults remain oblivious or uncaring of the extent to which their actions and behaviour is watched, mimicked and replicated by children, some other form of learning experience will be necessary to counteract the effects of adverse modelling.

Apart from observed examples and individual experience, a further problem is created by the fact that children have the ability to be spiteful, vicious and downright nasty. For many, if not most, sharing does not come naturally and children's inclination to perceive themselves as the centre of the universe can lead to actions which are extremely hurtful to others and to themselves. Without an understanding of the ability to make choices, rather than to react by instinct, a child can become a victim of its own frustrated ignorance.

Childhood is a phenomenon of recent centuries and in its present form, is a socially constructed state. The years defined as 'childhood', prior to attaining adult status, is a state of being created to enable a period of growth, learning, and experimentation. This assumes, in our society, a level of responsibility by parents or guardians for care, nurture and protection of the child during this time.

Precisely what constitutes adequate care, nurture and protection is a debatable point and a question of degree. As society evolves, attitudinal issues become even more complex. The persistent assumption that good parenting is a natural talent bestowed on all those who produce children, creates an impossible predicament for some parents and unhappy circumstances for many children. We could all benefit from the recognition that parenting is not a natural talent possessed by everyone and that 'learning for life' involves skills which need to be taught and acquired.

We urgently need to reassess the way we value our children and re-evaluate the purpose of childhood. Bullying must certainly be given due recognition as an aspect of childhood but should not be isolated from the larger issue. In our concern to understand more about the problem of bullying, it is important to ensure that this one aspect of childhood is not taken up as a single cause at the expense of others. This is not to deny the significance of the problem of bullying, but only to stress that an array of other implications are entangled with it.

One example of this is the childhood 'code of silence'. Sometime in the past, the idea that children should learn to keep secrets, should not be 'tell tales' or 'tittletattles' became a matter of honour for children. From a clinical research perspective this piece of folklore is unlikely to be accepted as a causal factor in the bullying issue. However, once learned and practiced through the experience of being bullied, being a bully or even being an on-looker to bullying practices, this 'code' can have very significant and dangerous implications.

Most definitions of bullying will describe the problem as a child to child issue. Without wishing to trivialise or minimise in any way the problem of child abuse, I would suggest that, from a child's point of view, abuse by adults is in some aspects not dissimilar to being bullied. This is particularly true in terms of the 'code of silence'. Some adults who hurt and abuse children use this 'code of silence' very skilfully for their own ends with disastrous results for the children. If children have not had experience of talking to adults about things that bother them, of being believed and having something done to resolve the problems that arise in their lives, they will be incapable of dealing with adults who try to bribe them into keeping 'a little secret'. Children who are incapable of dealing with peer group bullying and intimidation will stand little chance of dealing with such pressure from adults.

There are other 'rules' which contribute to children's vulnerability, such as obeying adults without question, being 'seen and not heard' and always 'doing as you're told'. Children who are polite and well mannered are much more agreeable to be with and are more likely to grow into socially acceptable adults. However, children need to understand that sometimes they can break certain 'rules' (without being castigated) particularly when their own safety is at risk.

We live in a complicated world and it is important that children understand the reasons why certain rules are necessary or desirable. They need explanations from adults to help them sort out what is really meant from what is said, particularly as adults constantly confuse children with mixed messages and examples justified by, 'Do as I say and not as I do!'

Children need to have confidence that there are adults around them who can be trusted — and that there are far more of them than the other kind. This trust will be tested in a multitude of ways and it is vital that adults are consistent, as children will draw comparisons and make judgements. How can we be dismayed when a child who is suffering for some reason does not share the fact, if, on previous occasions and in other circumstances, that child has experienced or witnessed a total lack of interest from adults?

Adults continually make judgements about what is important — according to their own scale of things. Telling a frightened child that 'you are being silly' will not earn the child's trust. Children need to believe that adults care, will listen and help them. Whether they are scared of the dark, being bullied at school, intimidated by a brother or sister, or threatened by an adult in some way, we must be told if we are to be able to help. Children need also to understand that they are not being cowardly and have no reason to feel guilty if they need to enlist the help of an adult for any reason. Many children do not have this reassurance or do not believe it to be true. As a result, adults who do care are not only unable to prevent problems arising but are disempowered of a curative role.

Preventative approaches

Happily, there is a growing awareness of the importance of listening to and talking with children. Many schools are recognising that the ability to 'get on with others' is not just a natural talent which some have and others do not and are actively promoting concepts which educate children in 'learning for life'. Childhood is the time to acquire survival skills and also to begin to develop a sense of responsibility and an understanding that the qualty of life is important to us, to society, and to the world. The establishment of schools' councils can be valuable in providing a structure through which children can raise and discuss issues and concerns with staff.

There is a growing realisation that dealing with the problems which manifest themselves during childhood is not sufficient. To quote one headmaster I met during my research into bullying: 'If you have to deal with the problem of bullying you have already failed'. Children 'pick on' other children because of their size, the fact that they wear funny shoes, their skin is a different colour, they are girls and not boys or vice versa. Children need to appreciate, understand, and accept that others may be different but that they too have rights. Ideally, they should learn how to get on with each other before they learn how not to.

Many schools have found conflict resolution strategies valuable in dealing with bullying and preventing or counteracting aggressive behaviour amongst children. Conflict is not in itself necessarily a bad thing; in fact, it is inevitable. Conflict can be a force for change from which progress and growth can evolve. However, it is necessary to learn how to handle conflict in a creative way if the outcome is to be beneficial. Through drama and role-play children can experiment with techniques to resolve conflict in the abstract. By practicing such techniques, they increase their ability to deal with difficulties when they arise.

The use of co-operative games with children is becoming more common. These games are not only fun but can be a useful way of expanding children's understanding of the value of interaction and interdependence. Such games use group exercises to develop trust, encourage strategic planning and working in unison (Herbert, Ch. 6).

Affirmation is also important. To feel positive about others, we need to feel positive about ourselves. Children can be encouraged in all kinds of ways to develop their self-confidence, self-respect and thereby their ability to respect others.

Under the broad heading of Human Rights and Peace Education, much has been achieved in the development of resources and materials to assist teachers and others who work with children. Many valuable initiatives are currently underway but they are fragmented and can be difficult to track down. The list of organisations and materials that follows is not exhaustive nor comprehensive but is aimed to assist those who wish to explore these areas in greater depth.

The problem of bullying will, no doubt, remain a feature of childhood. However, much could be achieved in minimising the scale of the problem and the effect it has on children by implementing a pro-active and positive approach to 'learning for life'. We need to re-assess the attitudinal environment in which children operate at home, at school and at play. Finally, perhaps, we adults should recognise that some degree of change in our attitude and approach to children and childhood is an essential ingredient to changing children's behaviour.

LIST OF RESOURCES

Organisations

Quaker Peace and Service,
Education and Advisory Programme,
Friends House,
Euston Road,
London, NW1 2BJ.
Tel: 01 387 3601

Provides advice on resources, methodology and possible ways of coping with problems on topics related to world development and environmental issues, human rights education, conflict resolution and the social skills required for greater personal awareness and affirmation. They also offer workshops and in-service training to facilitate problem solving through practical strategies for action and evaluation.

Kingston Friends Workshop Group,
Friends Meeting House,
78 Eden Street,
Kingston upon Thames,
Surrey, KT1 1DJ.
Tel: 01 547 1197

Has been conducting problem solving workshops with schools and other organisations since 1981. Their 'Life Skills Programme' is based on the belief that good relationships depend on Communication, Co-operation, and Affirmation. Workshops for teachers and others are available. The group has prepared a guidelines pack for schools wishing to set up 'Problem Management Groups'.

Quaker Peace Education Project,
Woodbrooke,
1046 Bristol Road,
Birmingham, B29 6LJ.

The above operates a resource base for the West Midlands area. Materials dealing with conflict resolution strategies, peace education and human rights can be viewed, borrowed and ordered. They also offer to work alongside teachers in the classroom to assist in implementing problem solving management structures and run workshops for teachers, parents and others.

Publications

Coping with Conflict. A resource book for the middle years by Frances Mary Nicholas. Published by Learning Developments Aids, Duke Street, Wisbech, Cambs. A manual which provides many activities and ideas. It is divided into four sections — Small World, Wider World, Others World and Our World. Each section develops the perspectives of children through drama, games and activities.

Getting on with Others. Published and supplied by The Woodcraft Folk, 13 Ritherdon Road, London, SW17. A development education resource pack for use with 6-9 year olds. It was originally developed for use by Woodcraft Folk groups but is also used in schools. It covers a wide range of topics including racism, sexism and bullying. Suggests strategies to encourage and develop greater personal confidence and self-esteem and a positive attitude towards others.

Let's Co-operate. Published by Peace Education Project and available from Mildred Masheder, 75 Belsize Lane, Hampstead, London, NW3 5AU. Offers strategies and activities under various headings — A Positive Self-Concept; Creativity; Communication and Co-operation amongst others. Intended for use by those who work with children between the ages of 3-11 years. Mildred Masheder also offers workshops for Nursery, Infant and Junior Teachers and parents. She may be contacted at the above address for further information.

Play the Game. Published and supplied by The National Coaching Foundation, 4 College Close, Beckett Park, Leeds, LS6 3QH. £1.00 plus p&p. Dealing mainly with sport this booklet aims to put 'winning' into perspective. It includes guidelines for everyone who may be involved in organising children's sports' activities.

Teaching Resources for Education in International Understanding, Justice and Peace. Published and supplied by Anne Brewer, 6 Phoenice Cottages, Bookham, Leatherhead, Surrey, KT23 4QG. £3.00 plus p&p. A comprehensive list of resource material across a wide range of topics, regularly updated. A library of all the materials is available at the same address.

Time to Talk. Produced by The Samaritans. This educational package includes a video and worksheets which aim to develop coping skills in secondary age children. The video raises a number of sensitive subjects such as bullying, extortion, racism, loneliness, relationship problems, family conflicts etc. Worksheets are provided to enable teachers and others to structure discussion groups around the various topics. Details of the package available from local branches of the Samaritans. The material is mainly for secondary aged pupils and costs £30.00.

Ways and Means. Published and supplied by Kingston Friends Workshop Group. (Address above). £4.50 plus p&p. This handbook contains activities and workshop ideas which have been used with children to enhance and enable creative thinking, co-operation, problem solving etc.

Winners All — co-operative games for all ages. Published and supplied by Pax Christi, 9 Henry Road, London, N4 2LH. Price £1.00 plus p&p. Over 50 games based on participation and co-operation rather than competition are described.

Notes

1. The Children's Play Unit, 16 Upper Woburn Place, London, WC1 0QP.
2. Learning Through Landscapes Project, Third Floor, Technology Home, Victoria Road, Winchester, SO23 7DU.

References

Moore, R. (1986) *Childhood's domain — Play and Place in Child Development*. Croom Helm.
Opie, I. and Opie, P. (1959) *The Lore and Language of School Children*. Oxford University Press.
Opie, I. and Opie, P. (1969) *Children's Games in Street and Playground*. Oxford University Press.
Rosen, M. (1985) *Kingfisher Book of Children's Poetry*. Kingfisher Books.
Sluckin, A. (1981) *Growin up in the Playground — The Social Development of Children*. Routledge and Kegan Paul.
Yule, V. (1985) 'Why are parents tough on children?' *New Society,* 73, 1187, 444-46.

Subject Index